THE DICTATORSHIP OF THE PROLETARIAT

The Dictatorship of the Proletariat

By

Karl Kautsky

Introduction by John H. Kautsky

Ann Arbor Paperbacks
for the Study of Communism and Marxism
The University of Michigan Press

Second printing 1971
First edition as an Ann Arbor Paperback 1964
Introduction copyright © by The University of Michigan 1964
First published by The National Labour Press Ltd., 1919
All rights reserved
ISBN 0-472-06096-1
Translated by H. J. Stenning
Published in the United States of America by
The University of Michigan Press and simultaneously
in Don Mills, Canada, by Longman Canada Limited
Manufactured in the United States of America

INTRODUCTION
By John H. Kautsky

Karl Kautsky's *The Dictatorship of the Proletariat* is a well-reasoned and strong plea to socialists to be faithful to democracy both before and after their expected advent to governmental power. As a result of a very common process whereby terms derived from the experience of Western politics come to refer to phenomena in quite different societies, to which their original meaning may be more or less irrelevant, the word "democracy" has in recent decades lost all meaning. There is now no type of society or government, no party or movement or ideology, including the communist ones, to which it has not been applied. When Kautsky wrote the present pamphlet, however, neither the conservative governing groups in his own Central Europe nor the Bolsheviks in Russia had yet laid claims to being democrats.

To Kautsky, then, democracy was a much more clearly defined concept and a much more controversial demand than it is to us. It meant to him, what it still vaguely means to most of us in the West, a system in which great masses of people participate in the political process, particularly through universal suffrage, and are enabled to do so through civil liberties such as freedom of speech, press, and organization. Those of us who are attached to this kind of system as most likely to assure a maximum of individual freedom can easily sympathize with Kautsky's values and associate ourselves with his side in his conflict with the Bolsheviks. However, as a plea for democracy and freedom, Kautsky's book speaks for itself and there is little need for me to call attention to its message. Any reader will find much in it of relevance to recent and present-day ideological conflicts and will shape his own attitude toward it accordingly.

Rather than engage in ideological conflict here, I propose to indicate briefly the place of Kautsky's pamphlet in the politics of the period and the function it served. I shall also critically examine some aspects of his work as a contribution to empirical social science apart from its value orientation. It seems both interesting and fair to do so, since, like most Marxist writings, Kautsky's book contains both normative discussion and empirical analysis. As is typically true of Marxian works, the two are often difficult to disentangle, but the empirical and analytical elements loom large in Kautsky's writings, for he was one of those Marxists who regarded himself above all as a social scientist rather than as a politician and had, in fact, ample justification for doing so.[1]

The social scientific emphasis of this Introduction is chosen on the assumption that most of the readers of this new edition of Kautsky's book will be quite different from those who read the original. There are few left who still want to refight the ideological battles of the period of the Russian Revolution. And those who fight ideological battles today are not likely to turn to Karl Kautsky's arguments for ammunition. To the communists, he remains a renegade and—in spite of his role as the chief defender of Marxism against Bernstein's Revisionism—has even become a Revisionist.[2] To most of those who choose to fight communism on ideological grounds, Kautsky will not appeal simply because he was a Marxist. The heirs of Kautsky's political tradition, the present-day socialist and social-democratic parties, have lost their attachment to Marxism and their interest in the kind of "theory" it stood for, as the groups they represent have become integrated into existing social and political systems.

The serious Marxist students of Marxism, as represented by such thinkers as Kautsky and Rudolf Hilferding, Max Adler, and Otto Bauer, have left the scene. The brilliant polemics of the first half-century after Marx's death, as carried on by Bernstein and Kautsky, Luxemburg, Lenin, and

Trotsky, degenerated into Stalin's heavy-handed
attacks on his enemies. They now find only a faint
echo in the dull disputations of the theoreticians of
Peking and Moscow. At last the field of Marxism
has been left to the social scientists. There has been
a remarkable growth of excellent scholarly litera-
ture on Marxism in recent years. It is both as an
object of social science study and as a contribution
to social science that I want to look at Kautsky's
pamphlet here.

A dozen years after the publication of *The
Dictatorship of the Proletariat* Kautsky described
the attitude he had held when writing the pamphlet
as follows:

If [the Bolsheviks] succeeded in making their
expectations and promises come true, it would
be a tremendous accomplishment for them and
for the Russian people and, indeed, for the
entire international proletariat. The teachings
of Marxism, however, could then no longer be
maintained. They would be proved false, but,
on the other hand, socialism would gain a
splendid triumph, the road to the immediate
removal of all misery and ignorance of the
masses would be entered in Russia and pointed
out to the rest of the world.

How gladly I would have believed that it
was possible! How gladly I would have been
persuaded! The most powerful, best-founded
theory must yield when it is contradicted by

the facts. However, they must be facts, not mere projects and promises.

Though still in doubt, I watched the Bolsheviks' first steps with benevolent expectation. I considered it impossible that they could immediately attain socialism, as they thought. Still, they were intelligent and knowledgeable people and they had acquired great power. Perhaps they would succeed in discovering new ways to raise the working masses from which the nations of the West, too, could learn.

However, my expectant benevolence did not last long. To my chagrin, I saw ever more clearly that the Bolsheviks totally misunderstood their situation, that they thoughtlessly tackled problems for the solution of which all conditions were lacking. In their attempts to accomplish the impossible by brute force, they chose paths by which the working masses were not raised economically, intellectually, or morally, but on the contrary, were depressed even deeper than they had been by tsarism and the World War.

Under these circumstances, I considered it incumbent on me to warn the Bolsheviks urgently against the road they had taken. I did this while the war was still in progress, in the summer of 1918, in my pamphlet "The Dictatorship of the Proletariat" (Vienna). I felt called upon to raise my warning voice all the

more as, next to the German and Austrian Social-Democrats, I stood—and still stand—in
closer relations with the Russian ones than
with any others.

In the most active contact with the Russian socialist emigrés since 1880, I had the
good fortune to gain as my friends the founders of Russian social-democracy, above all
Axelrod, but also Plekhanov, Vera Sassulich,
and Leo Deutsch. The members of the younger
generation of the Russian Social-Democrats
have done me the honor and given me the
pleasure of counting me, along with Plekhanov
and Axelrod, among their teachers.

Most of them also became my personal
friends, on the one side Martov, Dan, Abram-
ovich, etc., as much as on the other side Lenin,
Trotsky, Rakovsky, etc., with whom Parvus
and Rosa Luxemburg were at times closely
connected. In the closest and most active contact with my Russian friends and disciples,
which has now lasted for half a century, we
have mutually provided each other with intellectual stimulation. It is to this circum-
stance, above all, that I owe my insight into
Russian conditions.

Now the moment had come to render
thanks to my Russian friends for what I had
learned from them and to participate in their
intensive discussions of the road to be taken.

I did so to salve my conscience, not because I
expected any practical success. How could a
single German pamphlet in the midst of war,
published in Vienna, be effective in Petrograd
and Moscow! Most Bolsheviks did not even
hear of its existence. But even if they had
read my pamphlet, it was bound to remain in-
effective. They could no longer turn back
without abandoning themselves. The logic of
facts has always been stronger than the logic
of ideas.[3]

The Dictatorship of the Proletariat was the opening
gun in what became the greatest debate between
social-democratic and communist interpreters of
Marxism. Lenin replied to it in his famous *The
Proletarian Revolution and the Renegade Kautsky.*
Kautsky returned to his attack on the Bolsheviks
in *Terrorism and Communism.* Trotsky counter-
attacked in a pamphlet of the same name to which
Kautsky responded in his *Von der Demokratie zur
Staatssklaverei.*[4] To explain Kautsky's leading role
in this debate, I can do no better than to quote
from Max Shachtman's foreword to the new University of Michigan Press edition of Trotsky's contribution to the debate:

The choice of main target for the Bolshevik
barrage was not accidental. The leaders of the
Russian socialist opposition to the Bolsheviks
—the Mensheviks and the Social Revolutionists—were very little known to the mass of the

socialist movement outside of Russia; their writings were even less well known. The position of Kautsky was altogether different.

Karl Kautsky had known both Karl Marx and Friedrich Engels in his youth. After their death, he became the principal literary executor of the two founders of modern socialism. His writings on a wide variety of subjects were regarded everywhere as classical statements of the socialist view. He virtually founded and for thirty-five years edited the theoretical organ of the German Social Democracy, *Die Neue Zeit,* and it is no exaggeration to say that no other periodical had so profound an influence upon the whole generation of Marxists before World War I, not in Germany alone but throughout the world. In his own party and in the Socialist (the Second) International for most of its quarter of a century before the war brought about its collapse, he was unique in the prestige and authority in the sphere of Marxian theory that he enjoyed among socialists of all schools. His renown was scarcely diminished, at least up to the outbreak of the war, by occasional questioning of his Marxian orthodoxy by the small but more radical wing of socialism or by the fact that the actual political leadership of his party shifted steadily away from him. It is worth noting, too, that except for the Poles and of course the Russians, no one in the international socialist movement showed a greater interest, knowledge, and understanding of Russian problems under tsarism and of the Russian socialist movement than Kautsky. The Russian Marxists of all tendencies held Kautsky in almost awesome esteem. Up to August 1914, the writings of Lenin in particular are studded with the most respectful and even laudatory references to Kautsky, with whose views he sought to associate himself as much as possible and whose approval he, Lenin, adduced whenever he could as a most authoritative contribution to Russian socialist controversies.

. . . When the Bolsheviks took power in Russia . . . and Kautsky, not unexpectedly, promptly came forward as their opponent on an international scale, so to say, the breach between them became wide and deep and irreparable.

From the very beginning of the revolution, the Bolsheviks sought the active support of socialists outside of Russia, not only as sympathizers of the revolution they had already carried out but for the world revolution which was to be led by the Communist (the Third) International which they proposed to establish as quickly as possible. The opposition of a socialist of Kautsky's standing was therefore a matter of exceptional concern. Hence the vehemence, the intensity, and extensiveness, of Lenin's and Trotsky's polemics. . . .[5]

However, it was not only the Bolsheviks who opposed Kautsky. As he himself wrote:

Many of my political friends in Germany and Austria also disapproved of my stand against Bolshevism. They considered it possible that it would push through its program and demanded that it not be disturbed and discouraged in its efforts. Measures which I regarded as utterly wrong and as fatal mistakes appeared to them as mere blemishes, either the transient consequences of the war or the price that must be paid for every new experience— as infantile disorders of early youth.[6]

Under these circumstances, it took courage in socialist circles to attack Lenin when Kautsky did so. Having cut himself off from the German Majority Socialists during World War I because he refused to support the imperial government's war effort, he now isolated himself from many in his own Independent Social-Democratic Party. He was then one of the relatively few socialists, certainly among the Independents, who was not carried away by the general enthusiasm for the Bolsheviks, which has long been forgotten as a result of the sharp anticommunism of most social-democrats in the past forty years. Even the editor of the English translation of the present work as published in 1919 by the National Labour Press for the Independent Labour Party Library found it appropriate to write in his preface that the Bolsheviks had "accomplished wonderful achievements" and that "Lenin himself is the first to admit that they have made mistakes." He considered it necessary to say that he made "no apology" for the publication of *The Dictatorship of the Proletariat,* but, far from approving of it, merely pleaded the need for "impartiality and tolerance" as his reasons for the publication.

Kautsky's pamphlet was written in early August 1918, less than a year after the Bolshevik seizure of power in St. Petersburg and Moscow, after the conclusion of the Treaty of Brest-Litovsk, but before the end of World War I and before the revolutions in Germany and Austria. Kautsky expected these revolutions and wanted to prevent them from coming under communist influence. This was, indeed, one of the main purposes of his book (see particularly the final chapter which is directed against "The New Theory" of dictatorship on the Soviet pattern as an inevitable part of proletarian revolutions everywhere).

Immediately after the outbreak of the German Revolution in November 1918, a revised edition of Kautsky's pamphlet appeared in Berlin under the title *Demokratie oder Diktatur,* which omits the sections directly concerned with Russia (Chapters 1, 6, 7, 9, and 10) and substitutes a new first chapter. In it, Kautsky states that the Bolsheviks' call for dictatorship would not be taken seriously in the Western democracies, but that it had some appeal in Germany which, like Russia, had lived under a militarist and police autocracy.

Therefore it has become necessary to examine once again the problem of democracy in relation to the proletariat and to socialism, a problem that had appeared to us as well settled for decades. For this purpose I published a few weeks before the [German] Revolution a pamphlet entitled *The Dictatorship of the Proletariat* (Vienna: Volksbuchhandlung, J. Brand).

Its major part was concerned with Russian conditions. Everything I said on that subject has unfortunately been confirmed by the facts.

Today we have a revolution ourselves. Today we confront, not for Russia but for Germany, the question: dictatorship or democracy?[7]

To understand *The Dictatorship of the Proletariat,* one must not confuse the dictatorship Kautsky attacks with modern totalitarianism. In 1918 rival parties had been outlawed, the suffrage had been restricted, and open organized opposition had been suppressed by the Bolsheviks, but there was as yet not effective terror or propaganda or regimentation affecting the bulk of the population. At that time, modern totalitarianism, communist or Fascist, which has since shaped our concept of "dictatorship" was still unknown. Kautsky's image of dictatorship was hence quite different from ours. To him dictatorship was distinguished from democracy chiefly because it lacked universal suffrage and popular participation in politics, while we have come to know universal suffrage and mass participation as characteristics of modern totalitarianism. Similarly, Kautsky thought that dictatorship with its reliance on military suppression would lead to civil war unless there was total political apathy. He did not—and could not yet—understand that totalitarian methods can avoid both apathy and civil war.

In opposition to dictatorship, Kautsky (especially in Chapter 4) makes his case for a strong parliament as the only way to control the bureaucracy and the military, for universal equal suffrage, and for the protection of minorities and groups opposing the government. To appreciate Kautsky's emphasis on these, one needs to remember not only that his book was directed against Bolsheviks and at their followers and potential followers in Central Europe, but also that it was written in Berlin when the Prussian three-class suffrage and the German Empire with its bureaucracy and military unchecked by any effective parliament were still intact.

Kautsky suggested (in Chapters 6 and 7) that

the Bolsheviks should have followed democratic procedures. Thus, he felt that they should have accepted the constituent assembly elected by universal suffrage; that the soviets, as representatives of only part of the population, should not serve as governmental organizations; that the suffrage should be universal rather than limited to ill-defined categories of citizens, as it was in the early Soviet Republic; that opposition groups, including proletarian ones, should not be excluded from the soviets. In retrospect, all this may well appear to us as irrelevant. At the time, however, these statements served some functions. For one thing, they expressed Kautsky's bitterness and disappointment that a faction which had grown out of the Marxist movement—which to Kautsky was, above all, a democratic movement—should have abandoned the very goals for which he had by then fought for some forty years. Second, his words were to be a warning to other socialists, who were also attached to democratic values, not to follow Lenin. And, third, they served as a sharp polemical weapon to which Lenin was particularly vulnerable, because having used Marxian, i.e., Western democratic, symbols all along, he could now be accused of having betrayed his own past.

In our own time, the communists, whom Kautsky here accuses of betraying Marxism, have so successfully assumed its mantle that Marxism and communism are widely held to be identical and

most democratic socialists no longer lay claim to
the Marxian heritage. Kautsky's book now serves
as a useful reminder that, until less than half a
century ago, it was generally taken for granted
that Marxism stood for democracy. Only under
these circumstances could the Marxist Kautsky,
addressing himself chiefly to other Marxists, make
the Bolsheviks' abandonment of democracy his
principal charge against them.

One of the main bases of Lenin's claim that
the Bolshevik regime was Marxian in character lay
in his reference to the until then rarely used Marxian term "the dictatorship of the proletariat." Since
the Bolshevik claim has since been widely accepted,
it is not without interest to note that Kautsky (in
Chapter 5) could advance some good arguments
for his interpretation of the dictatorship of the
proletariat not as a form of government, but as a
condition which must necessarily arise where the
proletariat, being preponderant in numbers, has
conquered power and established democratic government.[8]

While any attempt to establish "what Marx
really meant" may seem to us both futile and, except from the point of view of the historian of ideas,
rather unimportant, it must not be forgotten that
Kautsky and Lenin were not engaged in a mere
scholarly dispute (though Kautsky, at any rate,
was sufficiently scholarly in temperament to regard
even this aspect of the conflict as important). The

stakes were not merely historical accuracy but political power. The authority of Marx was then still tremendous among the European socialist parties and particularly their intellectual elites. Whoever could claim that authority to support his position gained a political advantage. Until then, Kautsky had been widely regarded as the most authoritative interpreter of Marx's thought. He now sought to use that position to influence the European, and especially the German, socialist parties in favor of democracy and to minimize the Bolsheviks' appeal among them.

Lenin, on the other hand, insisted on his Marxian orthodoxy in the hope of winning over the European socialist parties (and again especially the German socialists) to support his revolution. In order to do so he had to destroy Kautsky's prestige as a Marxist. It was undoubtedly for this purpose, as well as to express his personal bitterness, that he employed an extremely abusive tone in his polemics with Kautsky.[9]

In Chapter 3 Kautsky lists the prerequisites of socialism: an interest on the part of the proletariat in socialism, superior proletarian numerical strength, and large-scale industry. All these are created only by advanced capitalism. Here Kautsky lays the groundwork for his orthodox Marxist attack on the Bolsheviks: that Russia was not "ripe" for socialist revolution. There is no question that on this central point Kautsky's interpretation of

Marx's materialist conception of history was right and Lenin's was wrong. Social classes and certainly the ideological superstructure cannot arise before the mode of production that gives rise to them; the gravediggers of capitalism cannot bury it before capitalism has created them.

But Kautsky did more than to repeat the elementary Marxian point that the socialist revolution and socialism can only be the product of, and hence must be preceded by, advanced capitalism. Far more than Marx and Engels, he stressed as prerequisites of socialism not merely those created by the growth of capitalism, but the "maturity" of the working class, which it acquires in the course of its conflicts with capitalism. By this he meant chiefly the organizational and intellectual advance of the workers. It results from the growth of mass labor organizations and a large-scale daily socialist press which are possible only under conditions of democracy; secret organizations and a few handbills are no substitute for them. Hence democracy emerges in Kautsky's thought as an essential prerequisite of one of socialism's essential prerequisites, the maturity of the proletariat: ". . . the more democratic a state is, the better organized and trained is its proletariat. Democracy may sometimes inhibit its revolutionary thought, but it is the indispensable means for the proletariat to attain that maturity which it needs to gain political power and carry through the social revolution."[10]

Before we criticize this conception in the light of historical evidence, it should be admitted that Kautsky does here usefully point to the link between the rise of democracy and that of the labor movement, each strengthening the other, for which there is much evidence in the history of some of the most industrialized countries.[11] Marx and Engels were by no means unaware of it, but died too soon to see it as clearly as Kautsky could, and Lenin, confronting the situation he did in Russia, had to deny it.

It is worth noting that Kautsky's insistence that the proletariat could rise to power only through the use of democratic procedures did not, as has often been asserted, make him a revisionist. The question whether socialism was to be attained by democracy or revolution was not an issue in Kautsky's famous controversy with Bernstein. Both stood for the achievement of socialism through democracy. The issue on which they differed was how to attain democracy, especially in imperial Germany. In *The Road to Power*,[12] generally—and even by Lenin—regarded as his most "revolutionary" anti-Revisionist work, Kautsky demanded only the democratization of the German government and implied that it could not be attained peacefully in view of the resistance of the German ruling classes.

What Kautsky wrote in 1918, then, is quite consistent with what he had been saying even before and during his controversy with Revisionism. His anti-Bolshevism was consistent with his anti-Revisionism, and both flowed from his conception of orthodox Marxism. It is significant that in *The Dictatorship of the Proletariat* some of his discussion of the role of democracy in the proletariat's rise to power takes the form of a long quotation from an article of his of 1893—when Kautsky was generally regarded as the leading theoretician of orthodox Marxism—an article which had been previously reprinted in his *The Road to Power* of 1909. On the other hand, it is also significant that in his present anti-Bolshevik work, Kautsky does not hesitate to reprint his earlier view that valuable as democracy is to the proletariat, it cannot remove the class conflicts of capitalist society or prevent the eventual inevitable overthrow of capitalism. Even in a democracy, the proletariat will not forego the social and political revolution—that is, the attainment of governmental power and the institution of socialist measures—but these are seen as peaceful processes. As Kautsky wrote in 1893: "This so-called peaceful method of the class struggle, which is confined to nonmilitary methods, parliamentarism, strikes, demonstrations, the press, and similar means of pressure, has the more chance of being retained in a country the more effective its democratic institutions are, the higher the state of political and economic understanding, and the self-control of the people."[13]

Kautsky's work rests on the Marxian conviction that the proletariat must conquer political power. He is certain (particularly in Chapter 2) that it will do so through democracy. All this is based on assumptions which have since proved wrong, assumptions of growing numbers and of growing alienation and exploitation of the workers and of their consequently growing class consciousness. We now know, as Kautsky did not and probably could not know, that the trend is the other way. For one thing, with mechanization increasing beyond a certain point, and especially with automation, the number of workers engaged in production declines. Second, growing industrialization and, in part, the very democracy Kautsky extolled as the road to power lead not to the "maturity" of labor that prepares it to take power and introduce socialism, but to less alienation, exploitation, and class consciousness, and hence workers become integrated into society instead of "conquering" it. To be sure, in this process, workers acquire more education, a higher standard of living, and, in many cases, also stronger organizations—all aspects of Kautsky's proletarian maturity. However, fewer and fewer of them—rather than more and more as Kautsky still took for granted—think of themselves as workers. Hence socialist parties in advanced industrial countries—the formerly Marxian German and Austrian ones no less than the British

Labour Party—have recently felt the need to broaden their appeal to go beyond the working class. It is fruitless to argue whether this development constitutes the victory of the proletariat or of the bourgeoisie. It is neither, because such Marxian categories are simply inadequate in an analysis of the history of the past half century in the most advanced countries.

Kautsky was by no means wholly unaware of the decline of class conflicts and of ideology in advanced democratic countries. In his 1893 article, which he quotes here, he spoke of "the democratic-proletarian method of struggle" being "duller" and "less dramatic" than the upheavals of the bourgeois revolutions, and he noted with irony, but not incorrectly, that some of the literary intelligentsia but not the workers would regret this. Kautsky also stated (in Chapter 4) that what he calls an interest in theory, a concern with the broad aspects of society, is a reaction to despotic regimes, to a situation in which only a small elite can be active in oppositional politics. Under democracy, greater masses are drawn into politics, more workers are involved in the administrative details of mass organizations, they become concerned with petty matters and momentary successes and develop opportunism and contempt of "theory." Today one may or may not share Kautsky's value judgment of the "true believer" as against the labor bureaucrat, but there is little doubt that he diagnosed the trend correctly. However, given his ideological position (which could be squared with reality much more easily half a century ago), Kautsky would only admit that it was a short-run trend, though it could last for years or even decades. Since even democracy could not remove the "contradictions" and conflicts of capitalist society, the workers—and now not merely the elite but the masses themselves (especially if labor time was reduced and free time increased)—would sooner or later necessarily face situations that would raise their minds beyond everyday problems and would kindle what he calls revolutionary thought and aspirations, i.e., those directed at a large-scale reorganization of society. Here ideology, as is so often true in Marxist thought, has, almost imperceptibly, taken over from social science.

According to Kautsky the proletariat needs democracy not only before its conquest of power but also afterward. He therefore attacks the concept of a dictatorship of the proletariat (especially in Chapter 5). There can, he points out, be no dictatorship of a class, but only of a party. If there are several proletarian parties, it will be a dictatorship of one over the others. If the one came to power as a result of an alliance with peasants, then the dictatorship is one of proletarians and peasants over proletarians.

To Kautsky, there is no reason why the proletariat should resort to dictatorship at all. It will ordinarily come to power only when it is in the great majority, and it would then be suicidal for it to give up democracy, for universal suffrage is its greatest source of moral authority. If a proletarian party did come to power without majority support —which Kautsky considered very unlikely in an advanced country—it could not maintain itself in power and realize its goals. It could not maintain itself through intellectual superiority, for as long as the majority of the population is opposed to socialism, most intellectuals will be, too. The alternative is the use of centralized organization and military power. It, however, is likely to produce civil war as a reaction, and it is impossible to reorganize society along socialist lines in the midst of war and especially under conditions of chronic civil war. If the proletarian revolution does involve civil war, socialists have an interest in keeping that war as brief as possible and having it serve only to establish democracy. The social revolution should then be carried out under democracy, for it must not at any time go farther than the majority will accept if it is to be permanently successful.

All this, of course, is based on Kautsky's conception of socialism:

> [It is] the organization of production by society. It requires economic self-government by the entire people. State organization of production by a bureaucracy or by dictatorship of a single stratum of the population does not

constitute socialism. It requires organizational experience of broad masses of the people, presupposes numerous free organizations, both economic and political, and needs the most complete freedom of organization. The socialist organization of labor must not be an organization along military lines.[14]

And, as Kautsky states categorically at the beginning of his pamphlet:

For us, therefore, socialism without democracy is unthinkable. We understand by modern socialism not merely social organization of production, but democratic organization of society as well. Accordingly, socialism is for us inseparably linked with democracy. No socialism without democracy.[15]

Once this conception of socialism is accepted, Kautsky's opposition to dictatorship follows naturally, and he wins his argument with Lenin hands down. As long as the socialist movement was largely a Western phenomenon and socialist parties in Eastern Europe were merely groups of intellectuals who had adopted the Western socialist doctrines, Kautsky's view was, in fact, very generally held, and he was perhaps justified in stating categorically what "socialism" was and what it was not.

With the Russian Revolution, the term "socialism" (much as has been true of the word "democracy") ceased to have a single meaning.

The problem Lenin confronted was, in fact, not the one that Marx had in mind: that of workers coming to power in an advanced capitalist country in order to transfer the means of production from private to public hands. It was an utterly different one we have since become familiar with in many underdeveloped countries, that of intellectuals coming to power in a largely agrarian country in order to industrialize it. But though the substance changed, the words did not, deceiving an entire generation. Once this is recognized, the argument about what constitutes socialism loses much of its interest, for it has become an argument about a word which no longer corresponded to any one thing.

Neither Kautsky nor Lenin could be aware of this. Hence each argues that what he advocates is socialism and what the other stands for is not "true" socialism. Today when not only Western European labor parties, but Mao and Castro, Nkrumah and Touré, Nasser and Nehru all stand for something they choose to call "socialism," it should be obvious that the term has become devoid of substantive meaning and might as well be discarded for analytical purposes. Not only was this not as clear in 1918 as it ought to be today, but the contestants in the dispute were engaged not only in analytical pursuits but in a struggle for power. They used the term socialism not merely as an analytical concept but as a symbol. Since it was

then in the European labor movement as it is to-
day among nationalist intellectuals in underdeveloped countries a powerful positive symbol, it became important for each side to lay claim to "true"
socialism and to expose the opponents' socialism as
"false."

Lenin could not afford to admit even to himself that Marxism, as a product of Western conditions, was largely irrelevant to his problems in
Russia, for Marxism was widely popular in his
circles as holding out the promise of a revolution
whose success was scientifically guaranteed.
Kautsky, on the other hand, like Marx himself a
Western-oriented thinker who looked to the history
of England and France as the model of social development, also saw the Russian Revolution in terms
of Marxian, i.e., Western, categories. Marx pro-
vides two categories for revolutions, the bourgeois
revolution and the proletarian revolution. Since
Kautsky saw clearly enough that the Bolshevik
Revolution was not proletarian in character, he
argued that it must be bourgeois (see especially
Chapters 8 and 9). It does not occur to Kautsky
that both categories are inapplicable in an underdeveloped country like Russia, with a small proletariat and hardly any bourgeoisie.

Industrialization comes to underdeveloped
countries by a very different process from that
which produced it in the West, on the initiative of
intellectuals operating through government owner-

ship or control of industry and agriculture,[16] intellectuals who are therefore neither private capitalists nor proletarians who expropriated such capitalists. Not once does Kautsky suggest that the Western pattern might not fit Russia; all his comparisons, even those regarding the peasantry, are with Western countries. Here his thought, like Marxian thought generally, and, indeed, almost all Western thought of the period, reveals its parochialism. It is only very recently that we have begun to recognize that the political development of the West with its peculiar institutions of capitalism and of democracy and its class structure and ideologies, far from being a model which the rest of the world will follow, is quite exceptional.

That Kautsky was unable to offer an adequate interpretation of the Russian Revolution and the communist regime is borne out by the fact that his predictions regarding its future course failed to be fulfilled. Yet, to write off *The Dictatorship of the Proletariat* simply as a failure even as an attempt at social science analysis—quite apart from the political impact the pamphlet may have had—would be grossly unfair.

Today, traditional aristocratic regimes all over the underdeveloped world are yielding to movements led by Western-educated intellectuals committed to rapid modernization of their backward societies by means of some government control of industry and agriculture and more or less totalitarian political methods. It is now relatively easy to place the Russian Revolution in the same category with these upheavals, and, indeed, some would go so far as to regard Soviet development as a relevant model for other underdeveloped countries.

Half a century ago, any such comparison was virtually impossible. What is now a world-wide process dominating the daily headlines had hardly begun as yet. Only the Chinese and Mexican revolutions preceded the Russian one in their outbreak, but their character as modernizing movements evolved slowly and was by no means clear in 1918. Besides, China and Mexico, like the underdeveloped world generally, were given very little attention in European political thinking.

Russia, on the other hand, was a European country, and its revolutionaries, being Western-influenced, had always used Western symbols to describe their movements. No wonder Kautsky was misled by these symbols to draw irrelevant parallels with the West, just as all too many are similarly misled today by the appearance of "socialism," "democracy," "nationalism," etc., all over Asia, Africa, and Latin America. Far from being alone in this respect, Kautsky shared his "Western" view of the Russian Revolution with virtually all of its interpreters of all political tendencies. To this day, we tend to think of the Russian Revolution as akin more to the English and especially the French one than to the revolutions in Mexico and Turkey, Guinea and Indonesia.[17]

Limited as Kautsky was by his own Western-Marxist categories, however, he at least never accepted the very common interpretation of the Russian Revolution, shared by the communists and many anticommunists, that it was a proletarian revolution and hence part of an international anticapitalist movement. He thus did his best to stop the spread of the widely believed myth of communist world revolution. Had his view been the common rather than the exceptional one, the vicious cycle of mutually self-fulfilling prophecies of those who acted to advance and those who sought to prevent this world revolution might not have been set in motion so effectively that it affects East-West relations to the present day.

From the very beginning of the Bolshevik seizure of power in Russia, Karl Kautsky saw clearly and stated courageously that it was not and could not be a proletarian or a socialist, i.e., Western anticapitalist, revolution. And, as the leading Marxist of his generation, he could authoritatively reject its claims to being Marxist as well. It is this message, delivered not as an impassioned plea to the emotions but as a calm and cool appeal to reason, that makes *The Dictatorship of the Proletariat*

an important document in the history of Marxism
and of the socialist movement and a milestone at
that point of its path where communism and democratic socialism parted ways.

Washington University, St. Louis

NOTES

1. For a brief biography of Karl Kautsky and a selected
bibliography of his works, see my article in the forthcoming new edition of the *Encyclopedia of the Social
Sciences*.

2. For an amusing example, see Li Fu, Li Ssu-wen, and
Wang Fu-ju, "On Kautskyism," *Hung-ch'i (Red Flag)*
(Peiping), No. 8–9, April 25, 1962, pp. 28–41, translated in Joint Publications Research Service (Washington: Department of Commerce), JPRS 13903, May 29,
1962, pp. 76–120, which not only makes Kautsky out
to be a revisionist, but also, by implication, the ideological ancestor of Khrushchev.

3. Karl Kautsky, "Die Aussichten des Fünfjahresplanes,"
Die Gesellschaft, VIII, No. 3 (March 1931), 255–64
(pp. 261–62). This article appeared in translation as the
preface to the English edition of Karl Kautsky, *Bolshevism at a Deadlock* (London: George Allen &
Unwin, 1931), pp. 7–23. It is, however, here translated
from the German original.

4. V. I. Lenin, *The Proletarian Revolution and Renegade
Kautsky* (New York: International Publishers, 1934).
Kautsky, *Terrorism and Communism* (London: The
National Labour Press, 1920; first German edition
June 1919). Leon Trotsky, *Terrorism and Communism*.

A Reply to Karl Kautsky (Ann Arbor: The University of Michigan Press, 1961; written in 1920). Kautsky, *Von der Demokratie zur Staatssklaverei. Eine Auseinandersetzung mit Trotzki* (Berlin: "Freiheit," 1921).

5. Trotsky, *op. cit.*, pp. v–vii.
6. Kautsky, "Die Aussichten des Fünfjahresplanes," pp. 262–63.
7. Karl Kautsky, *Demokratie oder Diktatur* (Berlin: Paul Cassirer, 1918), p. 8.
8. For other comments by Kautsky on the dictatorship of the proletariat, see his *Von der Demokratie zur Staatssklaverei*, pp. 38–43 and 83–84; *The Labour Revolution* (New York: Dial Press, 1925), pp. 59–89, where Kautsky takes issue with Lenin's *The State and Revolution;* and *Social Democracy versus Communism* (New York: Rand School Press, 1946), pp. 29–47.
9. The following are a few samples from Lenin, *The Proletarian Revolution and Renegade Kautsky:* "monstrous theoretical confusion," "a schoolmaster who has become as dry as dust," "tediously chews the cud," "twaddle," "this windbag," "monstrous distortion," "sophistry," "subterfuge," "a lackey of the bourgeoisie," "absolute nonsense and an untruth," "extreme stupidity or very clumsy trickery," (all from pp. 15–19), "It is impossible to ennumerate all the absurdities uttered by Kautsky, since every phrase he utters is a bottomless pit of renegacy" (p. 24), "oh, civilized belly-crawling and bootlicking before the bourgeoisie!" (p. 28).
10. P. 96. In quoting from *The Dictatorship of the Proletariat* I have sought to correct certain inaccuracies in the English translation. Unfortunately, it has not been possible to publish a revised and corrected version of the present translation which is marked by all too many mistakes.
11. Why this evidence is compatible with other evidence pointing to "working-class authoritarianism," i.e., the tendency of the lower classes to be extremist and intolerant, is explained by Seymour Martin Lipset, *Political*

Man. The Social Bases of Politics (Garden City, N. Y.: Doubleday & Co., 1960), pp. 97–130.

12. *The Road to Power* (Chicago: Samuel A. Bloch, 1909).
13. P. 37. The article quoted here, as is noted in the German original but not in the present English translation, is Kautsky, "Ein sozialdemokratischer Katechismus," *Die Neue Zeit*, XII/1 (1893), 361–70, 402–10. It was quoted at length by Kautsky in his *The Road to Power* in 1909 (and not in 1900, as the present translation states).
14. P. 51.
15. Pp. 6–7.
16. Kautsky's comments on agriculture and industry in the early Soviet state (in Chapter 9) are, of course, entirely outdated now, for these fields have undergone tremendous changes since then. His remarks on the socialization of agriculture, however, are still of some interest. He considers it impossible in backward Russia, because agriculture can only be socialized on the basis of large agricultural enterprises with a highly developed technology. Only then can such a new mode of production be so advantageous to the peasants that they would want to join the socialized enterprises. It does not even occur to Kautsky that force could be used to make the peasants join, as it was by Stalin a decade later. To Kautsky, socialization made no sense unless it improved the conditions of the workers involved. To Stalin, on the other hand, socialization served the goal of rapid industrialization, which, at least for a few decades, is not at all the same thing as the improvement of working and living conditions. Here again Kautsky saw the goals of the Bolsheviks through Western eyes. Twelve years later, at the beginning of the collectivization of agriculture in the Soviet Union, Kautsky still held that it was bound to fail because it was not accepted voluntarily by the peasants and because of Russia's technical backwardness. Kautsky, *Bolshevism at a Deadlock*, pp. 27–58.
17. This does not mean that the former view is less "cor-

rect" than the latter one. One chooses one's categories
of comparison depending on the subject to be investi-
gated. It is merely suggested that the aspects of the
Russian Revolution with which Kautsky was concerned
can be more adequately analyzed by comparison with
underdeveloped countries than with the West.

CONTENTS

The Dictatorship of the Proletariat

CHAPTER I.

THE PROBLEM.

THE present Russian Revolution has, for the first time in the history of the world, made a Socialist Party the rulers of a great Empire. A far more powerful event than the seizing of control of the town of Paris by the proletariat in 1871. Yet, in one important aspect, the Paris Commune was superior to the Soviet Republic. The former was the work of the entire proletariat. All shades of the Socialist movement took part in it, none drew back from it, none was excluded.

On the other hand, the Socialist Party which governs Russia to-day gained power in fighting against other Socialist Parties, and exercises its authority while excluding other Socialist Parties from the executive.

The antagonism of the two Socialist movements is not based on small personal jealousies : it is the clashing of two fundamentally distinct methods, that of democracy and that of dictatorship. Both movements have the same end in view : to free the proletariat, and with it humanity, through Socialism.   But the view taken by the one is held by the other to be erroneous and likely to lead to destruction.

It is impossible to regard so gigantic an event as the proletarian struggle in Russia without taking sides.   Each of us feels impelled to violent partisanship.   And the more so because the problem which to-day occupies our Russian comrades will to-morrow assume practical significance for Western Europe, and does already decisively influence the character of our propaganda and tactics.

It is, however, our party duty not to decide for one or the other side in the Russian internal quarrel before we have thoroughly tested the arguments of both.   In this many comrades would hinder us.   They declare it to be our duty blindly to pronounce in favour of the section now at the helm.   Any other attitude would endanger the Revolution, and Socialism itself.   This is nothing less than to ask us to accept as already proved that which is still to be examined, viz., that one of the sections has struck out in the right path, and we must encourage it by following.

We place ourselves, of course, by asking for the fullest discussion, already on the ground of democracy. Dictatorship does not ask for the refutation of contrary views, but the forcible suppression of their utterance. Thus, the two methods of democracy and dictatorship are already irreconcilably opposed before the discussion has started. The one demands, the other forbids it.

In the meantime, dictatorship does not yet reign in our Party; discussion amongst us is still free. And we consider it not only as our right, but as our duty to express our opinions freely, because an appropriate and fruitful decision is only possible after hearing all the arguments. One man's speech is notoriously no man's speech. Both sides must be listened to.

We will, therefore, examine the significance which democracy has for the proletariat—what we understand by the dictatorship of the proletariat— and what conditions dictatorship, as a form of government, creates in the struggle for freedom of the proletariat.

CHAPTER II.

DEMOCRACY AND THE CONQUEST OF POLITICAL POWER.

The distinction is sometimes drawn between democracy and Socialism, that is, the socialisation of the means of production and of production, by saying that the latter is our goal, the object of our movement, while democracy is merely the means to this end, which occasionally might become unsuitable, or even a hindrance.

To be exact, however, Socialism as such is not our goal, which is the abolition of every kind of exploitation and oppression, be it directed against a class, a party, a sex, or a race.

We seek to achieve this object by supporting the proletarian class struggle, because the proletariat, being the undermost class, cannot free itself without abolishing all causes of exploitation and oppression, and because the industrial proletariat, of all the oppressed and exploited classes, is the one which constantly grows in strength, fighting capacity and inclination to carry on the struggle, its ultimate victory being inevitable.   Therefore, to-day every genuine opponent of exploitation and

4

oppression must take part in the class struggle, from whatever class he may come.

If in this struggle we place the Socialist way of production as the goal, it is because in the technical and economic conditions which prevail to-day Socialistic production appears to be the sole means of attaining our object. Should it be proved to us that we are wrong in so doing, and that somehow the emancipation of the proletariat and of mankind could be achieved solely on the basis of private property, or could be most easily realised in the manner indicated by Proudhon, then we would throw Socialism overboard, without in the least giving up our object, and even in the interests of this object. Socialism and democracy are therefore not distinguished by the one being the means and the other the end. Both are means to the same end. The distinction between them must be sought elsewhere. Socialism as a means to the emancipation of the proletariat, without democracy, is unthinkable.

Social production, it is true, is also possible in a system other than a democratic one. In primitive conditions communistic methods became the basis of despotism, as Engels noted in 1875, when dealing with the village communism which has existed in India and Russia down to our own day.

Dutch colonial policy in Java for a long time based the organisation of agricultural production under the so-called " culture " system upon land communism for the profit of the government who exploited the people.

The most striking example of a non-democratic organisation of social work was furnished in the eighteenth century by the Jesuit State of Paraguay. There the Jesuits, as the ruling class, organised with dictatorial power the labour of the native Indian population, in a truly admirable fashion, without employing force, and even gaining the attachment of their subjects.

For modern men, however, such a patriarchal regime would be intolerable. It is only possible under circumstances where the rulers are vastly superior to the ruled in knowledge, and where the latter are absolutely unable to raise themselves to an equal standard. A section or class which is engaged in a struggle for freedom cannot regard such a system of tutelage as its goal, but must decisively reject it.

For us, therefore, Socialism without democracy is unthinkable. We understand by Modern Socialism not merely social organisation of production, but democratic organisation of society as well. Accordingly, Socialism is for us inseparably connected with democracy. No Socialism without democracy. But this proposition is not equally true if reversed. Democracy is quite possible without Socialism. A pure democracy is even conceivable apart from Socialism, for example, in small peasant communities, where complete equality of economic conditions for everybody exists on the basis of participating in privately owned means of production.

In any case, it may be said that democracy is possible without Socialism, and precedes it. It is this pre-Socialist democracy which is apparently in the minds of those who consider that democracy and Socialism are related to each other as the means to an end, although they mostly hasten to add that, strictly speaking, it is really no means to an end. This interpretation must be most emphatically repudiated, because, should it win general acceptance, it would lead our movement into most dangerous tracks.

Why would democracy be an unsuitable means for the achievement of Socialism?

It is a question of the conquest of political power.

It is said that if in a hitherto middle-class democratic State the possibility exists of the Social Democrats becoming the majority at an election, the ruling classes would make use of all the forces at their command in order to prevent democracy asserting itself. Therefore, it is not by democracy, but only by a political revolution that the proletariat can conquer the political power.

Doubtless, in cases where the proletariat of a democratic State attains to power, one must reckon with attempts of the ruling classes to nullify by violence the realisation of democracy by the rising class. This, however, does not prove the worthlessness of democracy for the proletariat. Should a ruling class, under the suppositions here discussed, resort to force, it would do so precisely because it feared the consequences of democracy. And its violence would be nothing but the subversion of democracy. Therefore, not the uselessness of democracy for the proletariat is demonstrated by anticipated attempts of the ruling classes to destroy democracy, but rather the necessity for the proletariat to defend democracy with tooth and nail. Of course, if the proletariat is told that democracy is a useless ornament, the needful strength for its defence will not be created.   The mass of the people are everywhere too attached to their political rights willingly to abandon them. On the contrary, it is rather to be expected that they would defend their rights with such vigour that if the other side endeavoured to destroy the people's privileges, a political overthrow would be the result.   The higher the prole-

tariat values democracy, and the closer is its
attachment to its rights, the more may one
anticipate this course of events.

On the other hand, it must not be thought that
the forebodings above mentioned will everywhere
be realised. We need not be so fainthearted. The
more democratic the State is, the more dependent
are the forces exerted by the Executive, even the
military ones, on public opinion. These forces
may become, even in a democracy, a means of
holding down the proletarian movement, if the
proletariat is still weak in numbers, as in an
agrarian State, or if it is politically weak,
because unorganised, and lacking self-conscious-
ness. But if the proletariat in a democratic State
grows until it is numerous and strong enough to
conquer political power by making use of the
liberties which exist, then it would be a task of
great difficulty for the capitalist dictatorship to
manipulate the force necessary for the suppression
of democracy.

As a matter of fact, Marx thought it possible,
and even probable, that in England and America
the proletariat might peacefully conquer political
power. On the conclusion of the Congress of the
International at the Hague in 1872. Marx spoke at
a meeting, and among other things said :

" The worker must one day capture political

power in order to found the new organisation of labour.   He must reverse the old policy, which the old institutions maintain, if he will not, like the Christians of old who despised and neglected such things, renounce the things of this world,

" But we do not assert that the way to reach this goal is the same everywhere.

" We know that the institutions, the manners and the customs of the various countries must be considered, and we do not deny that there are countries like England and America, and, if I understood your arrangements better, I might even add Holland, where the worker may attain his object by peaceful means.   But not in all countries is this the case."

It remains to be seen whether Marx's expectations will be realised.

There are certainly in the above named countries sections of the ruling classes whose inclinations to use force against the proletariat grow.   But, beside these there are other sections in whom the rising power of the proletariat gains respect and evokes a desire to keep it in good humour by concessions. Although the world war, for the period of its duration, has strictly confined the struggle of the masses for freedom everywhere, it has brought to the English proletariat a considerable extension of political power.   It cannot to-day be foreseen how democracy in the various States will influence the forms which the conquest of political power by the proletariat will take, and how far it will avert the use of violent methods from both sides and promote the use of peaceful means. In any case, the institution of democracy would not lose its importance. In a democratic republic, where the people's rights have been firmly established for decades, perhaps centuries, rights which the people conquered by revolution, and maintained or extended, thus compelling the respect of the ruling classes for the masses, in such a community the forms of transition would certainly be different from those in a State where a military despotism has been accustomed to rule by force, and hold the masses of the people in check.

For us the significance of democracy in the pre-Socialist period is not exhausted with the influence it may have on the forms of transition to a proletarian regime.   It is most important for us during this period, in so far as it bears on the ripening of the proletariat.

CHAPTER III.

DEMOCRACY AND THE RIPENING OF THE PROLETARIAT.

Socialism postulates special historical conditions, which render it possible and necessary. This is pretty generally recognised. Yet there is by no means unanimity amongst us as regards the conditions which must be fulfilled in order to make modern Socialism possible, should a country be ripe for it. This divergence on such an important question is not a calamity, and so far as it causes us to be occupied with the problem at the present time is a matter for rejoicing. We are obliged to consider this matter because, for most of us, Socialism has ceased to be something that must be expected in hundreds of years, as we were assured by many at the time of the outbreak of war. Socialism has become a practical question on the order of the day.

What, then, are the pre-requisites for the establishment of Socialism?

Every conscious human action presupposes a will. The Will to Socialism is the first condition for its accomplishment.

This Will is created by the great industry. Where small production is uppermost in a society, the masses of the people are possessors of the means of production. He who happens to be without property conceives his ideal to be the acquirement of a small possession. This desire may, in some circumstances, assume a revolutionary form, but such a social revolution would not have a Socialist character—it would only redistribute the existing wealth in such a manner that everyone would receive a share. Small production always creates the Will to uphold or to obtain private property in the means of production which are in vogue, not the will to social property, to Socialism. This Will first appears amongst the masses when large scale industry is already much developed, and its superiority over small production is unquestioned; when it would be a retrograde step, if it were possible, to break up large scale industry when the workers engaged in the large industry cannot obtain a share in the means of production unless they take on a social form; when small production, so far as it exists, steadily deteriorates, so that the small producers can no longer support themselves thereby. In this way the Will to Socialism grows.

At the same time, the material possibilities of its achievement increase with the growth of the large industry. The larger the number of producers, and the more independent of each other they are, the more difficult it is to organise them socially. This difficulty disappears in the measure in which the number of producers decreases, and the relations between them become more close and uniform. Finally, alongside of the will to Socialism, and its material conditions—the raw material of Socialism—the strength to realise it must also exist. Those who want Socialism must become stronger than those who do not want it.

This factor, too, is created by the development of the large industry, which causes an increase in the number of proletarians—those who have an interest in Socialism—and a decrease in the number of capitalists, that is a decrease as compared with the number of proletarians. In comparison with the non-proletarian classes, the small peasants and lower middle classes, the number of capitalists may increase for some time. But the proletariat increases more rapidly than any other class in the State.

These factors are the direct outcome of the economic development. They do not arise of themselves, without human co-operation, but they arise without proletarian co-operation, solely through the operations of the capitalists, who have an interest in the growth of their large industry. This development is in the first place industrial, and

confined to the towns.   The agrarian development
is only a weak echo of it.   Socialism will come from
the towns and from industry, but not from agriculture.   For its realisation yet another—a fourth—
factor is needful besides those already mentioned.
The proletariat must not only have an interest in the
establishment of Socialism, it must not merely have
the material conditions for Socialism ready to
hand, and possess the strength to make use of them ;
it must also have the capacity to retain its hold of
them, and properly to employ them.   Only then
can Socialism be realised as a permanent method of
production.

To the ripening of the conditions, the necessary
level of the industrial development, must be added
the maturity of the proletariat, in order to make
Socialism possible.   This factor will not, however,
be created by the efforts of the capitalist to obtain
rent, interest and profit, without the co-operation
of the proletariat.   It must, on the contrary, be
obtained by the exertions of the proletariat in
opposition to the capitalist.

Under the system of small production those
without property fall into two sections.   For one
of them, viz., apprentices and peasants' sons, their
lack of property is only a temporary condition.
The members of this class expect one day
to become possessors and have an interest

in private property. The other section of
the class without property are the vagabonds,
who are unnecessary and even harmful parasites on
society, without education, without self-conscious-
ness, without cohesion. When a chance offers
itself, they are quite ready to expropriate the
possessors, but they neither want nor are able to
construct a new social order.

The capitalist method of production makes use
of this propertyless class of vagabonds, whose
numbers assume large proportions in the beginning
of the capitalist system. Out of superfluous, even
dangerous parasites, they are transformed into the
indispensable economic foundations of production,
and therefore of society. Capitalism increases
their numbers and multiplies their strength, but it
exploits their ignorance, rawness and incapacity.
It even seeks to depress the working classes to their
level. By overwork, monotony and dulness of
toil, labour of women and children, capitalism even
presses the working classes below the level of the
former vagabond class. The impoverishment of
the proletariat increases in an alarming degree.

From it, however, the first striving towards
Socialism appears as an effort to make an end of the
growing poverty of the masses. It seemed, however, that this poverty must render the proletariat
for ever incapable of emancipating itself. Middle-

class sympathy must save it, and bring Socialism about.

It is soon apparent that nothing can be expected from this sympathy. Sufficient strength to accomplish Socialism can only be expected from those whose interests lie that way, that is the proletarians. But were not they perishing without hope?

Not all, in fact. There were particular sections which had shown strength and courage to fight against poverty. This small fraction would do what the Utopians were not capable of doing.

By a sudden stroke it would capture the powers of the State, and bring Socialism to the people. This was the conception of Blanqui and Weitling. The proletariat, which was too ignorant and demoralised to organise and rule itself, should be organised and ruled by a government comprised of its educated élite, something like the Jesuits in Paraguay who had organised and governed the Indians.

Weitling foresaw the dictatorship of a single person, who would carry through Socialism at the head of a victorious revolutionary army. He called him a Messiah.

" I see a new Messiah coming with the sword, to carry into effect the teachings of the first. By his courage he will be placed at the head of the revolutionary army, and with its help he will crumble the decayed structure of the old social order, and drown the sources of tears in the ocean of forgetfulness, and transform the earth into a paradise.''—(Guarantees of Harmony and Freedom.)

A generous and enthusiastic anticipation. It is based, however, solely upon the expectation that the revolutionary army will find the right man. But suppose one is not disposed to accept this belief in a coming Messiah, and holds the conviction that unless the proletariat can free itself Socialism must remain an Utopia?

In view of the fact that the proletariat has not attained to the capacity for self-government in any of the organisations with which it is concerned, is not the hopelessness of Socialism, in face of the impoverishment of the workers by capitalism, thereby demonstrated?

So it would appear.   Yet practice and theory soon showed a way out.   In England the industrial proletariat first became a mass movement, there it found some instalment of democratic rights, some possibilities of organisation and of propaganda, and was stirred into motion by being summoned to the aid of the middle class in the struggle with the nobles for the franchise.

Among the Trade Unions and the Chartists the beginnings of the Labour movement first arose, with the resistance offered by the proletariat to its impoverishment and disfranchisement. It commenced its strikes, and its great fight for the suffrage and the normal working day.

Marx and Engels early recognised the significance of this movement. It was not the " theory of impoverishment " which characterised Marx and Engels. They held this in common with other Socialists, but were superior to them by not only recognising the capitalist tendency towards impoverishment, but also the proletarian counter tendency, and in this, in the class struggle, they recognised the great factor which would uplift the proletariat, and give it the capacity which it needs if it is not merely to grasp political power by the luck of an accident, but is to be in a position to make itself master of that power, and to use it.

The proletarian class struggle, as a struggle of the masses, presupposes democracy. If not absolute and pure democracy, yet so much of democracy as is necessary to organise masses, and give them uniform enlightenment. This cannot be adequately done by secret methods. A few fly sheets cannot be a substitute for an extensive daily Press. Masses cannot be organised secretly, and, above all, a secret organisation cannot be a democratic one. It always leads.to the dictatorship of a single man, or of a small knot of leaders. **The** ordinary members can only become instruments for carrying out orders. Such a method may be rendered necessary for an oppressed class in the absence of democracy, but it would not promote the self-government and independence of the masses. Rather would it further the Messiah-consciousness of leaders, and their dictatorial habits.

The same Weitling, who gave such prominence to the function of a Messiah, spoke most contemptuously of democracy.

"Communists are still pretty undecided about the choice of their form of government. A large part of those in France incline to a dictatorship, because they well know that the sovereignty of the people, as understood by republicans and politicians, is not suited for the period of transition from the old to a completely new organisation. Owen, the chief of the English Communists, would have the performance of specified duties allotted to men according to age, and the chief leaders of a government would be the oldest members of it. All Socialists with the exception of the followers of Fourier, to whom all forms of government are the same, are agreed that the form of government which is called the sovereignty of the people is a very unsuitable, and even dangerous, sheet anchor for the young principle of Communism about to be realised."

Weitling goes further. He will have nothing of democracy, even in a Socialist community.

'' If the idea of the sovereignty of the people is to be applied, all must rule.   This can never be the case, and it is, therefore, not the sovereignty of the people, but the chance sovereignty of some of the people.''

Weitling wanted the greatest geniuses to govern. They would be selected in a competition by scientific assemblies.

I have quoted Weitling in detail in order to show that the contempt for democracy, which is now recommended to us as the highest wisdom, is quite an old conception, and corresponds to a primitive stage in the working-class movement. At the same time that Weitling poured scorn on Universal Suffrage and freedom of the Press, the workers of England were fighting for these rights, and Marx and Engels ranged themselves by their side.

Since then the working classes of the whole of Europe, in numerous—often bloody—struggles, have conquered one instalment of democracy after the other, and by their endeavours to win, maintain and extend democracy, and by constantly making use of each instalment for organisation, for propaganda, and for wresting social reforms, have they grown in maturity from year to year, and from

the lowest have become the highest placed section
of the masses of the people.

Has the proletariat already attained the maturity
which Socialism postulates?   And are the other
conditions now in existence?   These questions are
to-day much disputed, the answers given being by
some as decisively in the affirmative as by others in
the negative.   Both answers seem to me rather
over hasty.   Ripeness for Socialism is not a condition which lends itself to statistical calculation
before the proof can be put to the test.   In any
case, it is wrong, as so often happens in discussing
this question, to put the material pre-requisites of
Socialism too much in the foreground.   No doubt,
without a certain development of the large industry
no Socialism is possible, but when it is asserted that
Socialism would only become practicable when
capitalism is no more in a position to expand, all
proof of this is lacking.   It is correct to say that
Socialism would be the more easily realisable the
more developed the large industry is, and therefore
the more compact the productive forces are which
must be socially organised.

Yet this is only relevant to the problem, when it
is considered from the standpoint of a particular
State.   The simplification of the problem in this
form is, however, counteracted by the fact that the
growth of the large industry is accompanied by an

expansion of its markets, the progress of the division of labour and of international communications, and therewith the constant widening and increasing complication of the problem of the social organisation of production. There is, indeed, no reason for believing that the organisation of the largest part of production for social ends, by the State, Municipalities, and Co-operative Societies, is not already possible in modern industrial States, with their banking facilities and their machinery for the conduct of businesses.

The decisive factor is no longer the material, but the personal one. Is the proletariat strong and intelligent enough to take in hand the regulation of society, that is, does it possess the power and the capacity to transfer democracy from politics to economics? This cannot be foretold with certainty. The factor in question is one which is in different stages of development in different countries, and it fluctuates considerably at various times in the same country. Adequate strength and capacity are relative conceptions. The same measure of strength may be insufficient to-day, when the opponents are strong, but to-morrow quite adequate, when they have suffered a moral, economic or military collapse.

The same measure of capacity might be quite inadequate to-day should power be attained in a highly complicated situation, and yet to-morrow it could be equal to all demands made on it, if meanwhile conditions have simplified and become stabler.

In every case only practice can show if the proletariat is already sufficiently mature for Socialism. We can only say the following for certain. The proletariat grows always in numbers, strength and intelligence, it is ever approaching the climax of its development.

It is not definite enough to say that the latter phase will be reached when the proletariat forms the majority of the people, and when the majority announce their adhesion to Socialism. On the other hand, it may be confidently said that a people is not yet ripe for Socialism so long as the majority of the masses are hostile to Socialism, and will have nothing of it.

So here again democracy not only matures the proletariat the soonest, but gives the quickest indications of this process.

CHAPTER IV.

The Effects of Democracy.

The modern State is a rigidly centralised organism, an organisation comprising the greatest power within modern society, and influencing in the most effective way the fate of each individual, as is especially obvious in time of war.

The State is to-day what the family and community used to be for the individual. If communities were in their way democratically organised, the power of the State, on the contrary, including the bureaucracy and the army, looms over the people, even gaining such strength that at times it acquires an ascendancy over the classes which are socially and economically dominant, thus constituting itself an absolute government. Yet this latter condition is nowhere lasting. The absolute rule of bureaucracy leads to its ossification and its absorption into endless time-wasting formulæ, and that just at the time when industrial capitalism is developing, when the revolutionary methods of production which arise from it subject all economic and social conditions to constant change, and impart a quicker movement to industrial life, thus requiring the speediest political adjustments.

The absolute rule of bureaucracy, therefore, leads to arbitrariness and stultification, but a system of production like capitalism, in which each producer is dependent upon numerous others needs for its prosperity the security and legality of social relations. The absolute State gets into conflict with the productive forces, and becomes a fetter on them. It is, then, urgently necessary for the executive to be subjected to public criticism, for free organisations of citizens to counterbalance the power of the State, for self-government in municipalities and provinces to be established, for the power of law-making to be taken from the bureaucracy, and put under the control of a central assembly, freely chosen by the people, that is a Parliament. The control of the Government is the most important duty of Parliament, and in this it can be replaced by no other institution. It is conceivable, though hardly practicable, for the law-making power to be taken from the bureaucracy, and entrusted to various committees of experts, which would draft the laws and submit them to the people for their decision. The activities of the executive can only be supervised by another central body, and not by an unorganised and formless mass of people.

The attempts to overcome the absolute power of
the State, as here described, are made by all classes
in a modern State, with the exception of those
which may share in its power, that is all except
bureaucrats, court nobles, the State Church, as well
as the great bankers who do a lucrative business
with the State.

Before the united pressure of the other classes,
which may include the landed gentry, the lower
clergy, the industrial capitalists, the absolute
regime must give way. In a greater or lesser
degree it must concede freedom of the Press, of
public meeting, of organisation, and a Parliament.
All the States of Europe have successfully passed
through this development.

Every class will, however, endeavour to shape
the new form of the State in a manner corresponding to its particular interests. This attempt is
especially manifested in the struggle over the
character of the Parliament, that is in the fight for
the franchise. The watchword of the lower classes,
of the people, is Universal Suffrage. Not only the
wage-earner, but the small peasant and the lower
middle classes have an interest in the franchise.

Everywhere and under all circumstances these
classes form the great majority of the population.
Whether the proletariat is the predominant class
amongst these depends on the extent of the

economic development, although this factor does not determine whether the proletariat comprises the majority of the population. The exploiters are always a small minority of the population.

In the long run no modern State can withstand the pressure of these classes, and anything short of general suffrage in our society to-day would be an absurdity. In capitalist society, with its constantly changing conditions, the classes cannot be stereotyped in fixed grooves. All social conditions are in a state of flux. A franchise based on status is consequently excluded. A class which is not organised as such is a formless fluctuating mass, whose exact boundaries it is quite impossible to mark. A class is an economic entity, not a legal one. Class-membership is always changing. Many handworkers who, under the regime of small industry, think they are possessors, feel like proletarians under large industry, and are really proletarians even when for purposes of statistics they are included with the possessing classes and independent producers. There is also no franchise based on the census which would secure to the possessing classes a lasting monopoly of Parliament. It would be upset by every depreciation in money values. Finally, a franchise based on education would be even more futile, in view of the progress of culture amongst the masses. Thus various

factors combine to render general suffrage the only
solution in the society of to-day, and bring the
question more and more to the front.   Above all,
it is the only rational solution from the standpoint
of the proletariat as the lowest class of the population. The most effective weapon of the proletariat
is its numerical strength.   It cannot emancipate
itself until it has become the largest class of the
population, and until capitalist society is so far
developed that the small peasants and the lower
middle classes no longer overweight the proletariat.

The proletariat has also an interest in the fact
that the suffrage should not only be universal and
equal, but also non-discriminatory, so that men and
women, or wage earners and capitalists, do not vote
in separate sections.   Such a method would not
only involve the danger that particular sections, who
belong to the proletariat in reality, but are not wage
earners in form, would be separated from it, but
it would also have the still worse result of narrowing
the outlook of the proletariat.   For its great
historical mission consists in the fact that the
collective interests of society fall into line with its
permanent class interests, which are not always the
same thing as special sectional interests.   It is a
symptom of the maturity of the proletariat when its
class consciousness is raised to the highest point by

its grasp of large social relations and ends.   This understanding is only made completely clear by scientific Socialism, not only by theoretical teaching, but by the habit of regarding things as a whole instead of looking at special interests which are furthered and extended by engaging in political action.   Confining the outlook to trade interests narrows the mind, and this is one of the drawbacks to mere Trade Unionism.   Herein lies the superiority of the organisation of the Social Democratic Party, and also the superiority of a nondiscriminatory, as compared with a franchise which divides the electors into categories.

In the struggle for the political rights referred to modern democracy arises, and the proletariat matures.   At the same time a new factor appears, viz., the protection of minorities, the opposition in the State.   Democracy signifies rule of majority, but not less the protection of minorities.

The absolute rule of bureaucracy strives to obtain for itself permanency.   The forcible suppression of all opposition is its guiding principle.   Almost everywhere it must do this to prevent its power being forcibly broken.   It is otherwise with democracy, which means the rule of majorities. But majorities change.   In a democracy no regime can be adapted to long duration.

Even the relative strength of classes is not a fixed

quantity, at least in the capitalist era.   But the strength of parties changes even quicker than the strength of classes, and it is parties which aspire to power in a democracy.

It must not here be forgotten, what so often happens, that the abstract simplification of theory, although necessary to a clear understanding of realities is only true in the last resort, and between it and actualities there are many intervening factors.   A class can rule, but not govern, for a class is a formless mass, while only an organisation can govern.   It is the political parties which govern in a democracy.   A party is, however, not synonymous with a class, although it may, in the first place, represent a class interest.   One and the same class interest can be represented in very different ways, by various tactical methods. According to their variety, the representatives of the same class interests are divided into different parties.   Above all, the deciding factor is the position in relation to other classes and parties. Only seldom does a class dispose of so much power that it can govern the State by itself.   If a class attains power, and finds that it cannot keep it by its own strength, it seeks for allies.   If such allies are forthcoming, various opinions and standpoints prevail amongst the representatives of the dominant class interests.

In this way, during the eighteenth century Whigs and Tories represented the same landed interest, but one party endeavoured to further it by alliance with the middle classes of the towns at the expense of the Throne and its resources, while the other party conceived the Monarchy to be its strongest support. Similarly to-day in England and also elsewhere, Liberals and Conservatives represent the same capitalist interests. But the one thinks they will be best served by an alliance with the landed class, and forcible suppression of the working classes, while the other fears dire consequences from this policy, and strives to conciliate the working classes by small concessions at the expense of the landed class.

As with the socially and economically ruling classes and their parties, so it is with the aspiring class and its parties.

Parties and classes are therefore not necessarily coterminous. A class can split up into various parties, and a party may consist of members of various classes. A class may still remain the rulers, while changes occur in the governing party, if the majority of the ruling class considers the methods of the existing governing party unsuitable, and that of its opponents to be more appropriate.

Government by parties in a democracy changes more rapidly than the rule of classes. Under these circumstances, no party is certain of retaining power, and must always count on the possibility of being in the minority, but by virtue of the nature of the State no party need remain in a minority for ever.

These conditions account for the growing practice of protecting minorities in a democracy.   The deeper the roots which a democracy has struck, and the longer it has lasted and influenced political customs, the more effective is the minority, and the more successfully it can oppose the pretensions of any party which seeks to remain in power at all costs.

What significance the protection of minorities has for the early stages of the Socialist Party, which everywhere started as a small minority, and how much it has helped the proletariat to mature, is clear.   In the ranks of the Socialist Party the protection of minorities is very important.   Every new doctrine, be it of a theoretical or a tactical nature, is represented in the first place by minorities.   If these are forcibly suppressed, instead of being discussed, the majority is spared much trouble and inconvenience.   Much unnecessary labour might be saved—a doctrine does not mean progress because it is new and championed by a minority.   Most of what arises as new thought has already been discussed long before, and recognised as untenable, either by practice or by refutation.

Ignorance is always bringing out old wares as if they were something new. Other new ideas may be original, but put in a perverted shape. Although only a few of the new ideas and doctrines may spell real progress, yet progress is only possible through new ideas, which at the outset are put forward by minorities. The suppression of the new ideas of minorities in the Party would only cause harm to the proletarian class struggle, and an obstacle to the development of the proletariat. The world is always bringing us against new problems, which are not to be solved by the existing methods.

Tedious as it may be to sift the wheat from the chaff, this is an unavoidable task if our movement is not to stagnate, and is to rise to the height of the tasks before it. And what is needful for a party is also needful for the State. Protection of minorities is an indispensable condition for democratic development, and no less important than the rule of the majority.

Another characteristic of democracy is here brought in view, which is the form it gives to the class struggle.

In 1893 and in 1900 I have already discussed this matter, and give below some quotations from my writings :

" Freedom of combination and of the Press and universal suffrage (under circumstances, even conscription) are not only weapons which are secured to the proletariat in the modern State by the revolutionary struggle of the middle class, but these institutions throw on the relative strength of parties and classes, and on the mental energy which vitalises them a light which is absent in the time of Absolutism. At that time the ruling, as well as the revolutionary, classes were fighting in the dark. As every expression of opposition was rendered impossible, neither the Government nor the Revolutionists were aware of their strength. Each of the two sides was thus exposed to the danger of over-estimating its strength, so long as it refrained from measuring itself in a struggle with the opponent, and of under-estimating its strength the moment it suffered a single defeat, and then threw its arms away.

" This is really one of the chief reasons why, in the revolutionary period of the middle class, so many institutions collapsed at one blow, and so many governments were overthrown at a single stroke, and it also explains all the vicissitudes of revolution and counter-revolution.

" It is quite different to-day, at least in countries which possess some measure of democratic government. These democratic institutions have been called the safety valve of society. It is quite false to say that the proletariat in a democracy ceases to be revolutionary, that it is contented with giving public expression to its indignation and its sufferings, and renounces the idea of social and political revolution. Democracy cannot remove the class antagonisms of capitalist society, nor prevent the overthrow of that society, which is their inevitable outcome. But if it cannot prevent the Revolution, it can avoid many reckless and premature attempts at revolution, and render many revolutionary movements unnecessary. It gives a clear indication of the relative strength of classes and parties; it does not do away with their antagonism, nor does it avoid the ultimate outcome of their struggle, but it serves to prevent the rising classes from attempting tasks to which they are not equal, and it also restrains the ruling classes from refusing concessions when they no longer have the strength to maintain such refusal. The direction of evolution is not thereby altered, but the pace is made more even and steady. The coming to the front of the proletariat in a State with some measure of democratic government will not be marked by such a striking victory as attended the middle classes in their revolutionary period, nor will it be exposed to a violent overthrow.

"Since the rise of the modern Social Democratic

working-class movement in the sixties, the European proletariat has only suffered one great defeat, in the Paris Commune of 1871. At the time France was still suffering from the consequences of the Empire, which had withheld real democratic institutions from the people, the French proletariat had only attained to the slightest degree of class-consciousness, and the revolt was provoked.

"The proletarian-democratic method of conducting the struggle may seem to be a slower affair than the revolutionary period of the middle class; it is certainly less dramatic and striking, but it also exacts a smaller measure of sacrifice. This may be quite indifferent to the finely endowed literary people who find in Socialism an interesting pastime, but not to those who really carry on the fight.

"This so-called peaceful method of the class struggle, which is confined to non-militant methods, Parliamentarism, strikes, demonstrations, the Press, and similar means of pressure, will retain its importance in every country according to the effectiveness of the democratic institutions which prevail there, the degree of political and economic enlightenment, and the self-mastery of the people.

"On these grounds, I anticipate that the social revolution of the proletariat will assume quite other forms than that of the middle class, and that it will be possible to carry it out by peaceful economic, legal and moral means, instead of by physical force, in all places where democracy has been established.''

The above is my opinion to-day.

Of course, every institution has its bad side, and disadvantages can be discovered in democracy.

Where the proletariat is without rights, it can develop no mass organisation, and normally cannot promote mass action; there it is only possible for a handful of reckless fighters to offer lasting opposition to the governing regime.   But this élite is daily confronted with the necessity of bringing the entire system to an end.   Undistracted by the small demands of daily politics, the mind is concentrated on the largest problems, and learns constantly to keep in view the entire political and social relations.

Only a small section of the proletariat takes part in the fight, but it cherishes keen theoretical interest, and is inspired by the great aims.

Quite differently does democracy affect the proletariat, when it has only a few hours a day at its disposal under present-day conditions.   Democracy develops mass organisations involving immense administrative work; it calls on the citizen to discuss and solve numerous questions of the day, often of the most trivial kind. The whole of the free time of the proletariat is more and more taken up with petty details, and its attention occupied by passing events. The mind is contracted within a narrow circle. Ignorance and even contempt of theory, opportunism in place of broad principles, tend to get the upper hand. Marx and Engels praised the theoretical mind of the German working class, in contrast with the workers of Western Europe and America. They would to-day find the same theoretical interest amongst the Russian workers, in comparison with the Germans.

Nevertheless, everywhere the class-conscious proletariat and their representatives fight for the realisation of democracy, and many of them have shed their life's blood for it.

They know that without democracy nothing can be done. The stimulating results of the struggle with a despotism are confined to a handful, and do not touch the masses. On the other hand, the degenerating influence of democracy on the proletariat need not be exaggerated. Often is it the consequence of the lack of leisure from which the proletariat suffers, not of democracy itself.

It were indeed extraordinary if the possession of freedom necessarily made men more narrow and trivial than its absence. The more democracy tends to shorten the working day, the greater the sum of leisure at the disposal of the proletariat, the more it is enabled to combine devotion to large problems with attention to necessary detail. And the impulse thereto is not lacking. For whatever democracy may be able to accomplish it cannot resolve the antagonisms inherent in a capitalist system of production, so long as it refrains from altering this system. On the contrary, the antagonisms in capitalist society become more acute and tend to provoke bigger conflicts, in this way forcing great problems on the attention of the proletariat, and taking its mind off routine and detail work.

Under democracy this moral elevation is no longer confined to a handful, but is shared in by the whole of the people, who are at the same time gradually accustomed to self-government by the daily performance of routine work.

Again, under democracy, the proletariat does not always think and talk of revolution, as under despotism. It may for years, and even decades, be immersed in detail work, but everywhere situations must arise which will kindle in it revolutionary thought and aspirations.

When the people are roused to action under a democracy, there is less danger than under despotism that they have been prematurely provoked, or will waste their energy in futile efforts. When victory is achieved, it will not be lost, but successfully maintained.   And that is better in the end than the mere nervous excitement of a fresh revolutionary drama.

CHAPTER V.

DICTATORSHIP.

DEMOCRACY is the essential basis for building up a Socialist system of production. Only under the influence of democracy does the proletariat attain that maturity which it needs to be able to bring about Socialism, and democracy supplies the surest means for testing its maturity. Between these two stages, the preparation for Socialism and its realisation, which both require democracy, there is the transition state when the proletariat has conquered political power, but has not yet brought about Socialism in an economic sense. In this intervening period it is said that democracy is not only unnecessary, but harmful.

This idea is not new. We have already seen it to be Weitling's. But it is supposed to be supported by Karl Marx. In his letter criticising the Gotha party programme, written in May, 1875, it is stated: "Between capitalist and communist society lies the period of the revolutionary transformation of the one into the other. This requires a political transition stage, which can be nothing

42

else than the revolutionary dictatorship of the proletariat.''

Marx had unfortunately omitted to specify more exactly what he conceived this dictatorship to be. Taken literally, the word signifies the suspension of democracy. But taken literally it also means the sovereignty of a single person, who is bound by no laws. A sovereignty which is distinguished from a despotism by being regarded as a passing phase, required by the circumstances of the moment, and not a permanent institution of the State.

The expression '' Dictatorship of the Proletariat.'' that is the dictatorship not of a single person, but of a class, excludes the inference that Marx thought of dictatorship in the literal sense.

He speaks in the passage above quoted not of a form of government, but of a condition which must everywhere arise when the proletariat has conquered political power. That he was not thinking of a form of government is shown by his opinion that in England and America the transition might be carried out peacefully. Of course, Democracy does not guarantee a peaceful transition. But this is certainly not possible without Democracy.

However, to find out what Marx thought about the dictatorship of the proletariat, we need not have recourse to speculation. If in 1875 Marx did not explain in detail what he understood by the dictatorship of the proletariat, it might well have been because he had expressed himself on this matter a few years before, in his study of the Civil War in France.   In that work, he wrote : " The Commune was essentially a government of the working class, the result of the struggle of the producing class against the appropriating class, the political form under which the freedom of labour could be attained being at length revealed."

Thus the Paris Commune was, as Engels expressly declared in his introduction to the third edition of Marx's book, " The Dictatorship of the Proletariat."

It was, however, at the same time not the suspension of democracy, but was founded on its most thoroughgoing use, on the basis of universal suffrage.   The power of the Government was subjected to universal suffrage.

" The Commune was composed of town councillors, chosen by general suffrage in the various departments of Paris.

"Universal suffrage was to serve the people, constituted in Communes, as individual suffrage serves every other employer in the search for the workmen and managers in his business."

Marx constantly speaks here of the general suffrage of the whole people, and not of the votes of a specially privileged class. The dictatorship of the proletariat was for him a condition which necessarily arose in a real democracy, because of the overwhelming numbers of the proletariat.

Marx must not, therefore, be cited by those who support dictatorship in preference to democracy. Of course, this does not prove it to be wrong. Only, it must be demonstrated on other grounds.

In the examination of this question, dictatorship as a condition must not be confused with dictatorship as a form of government, which alone is a subject of dispute in our ranks. Dictatorship as a form of government means disarming the opposition, by taking from them the franchise, and liberty of the Press and combination. The question is whether the victorious proletariat needs to employ these measures, and whether Socialism is only or most easily realisable with their aid.

It must next be noted that when we speak of dictatorship as a form of government, we cannot mean the dictatorship of a class. For, as already remarked, a class can only rule, not govern. If by dictatorship we do not merely signify a state of sovereignty, but a form of government, then dictatorship comes to mean that of a single person, or of an organisation, not of the proletariat, but of a proletarian party. The problem is then complicated so soon as the proletariat itself is divided

into various parties.   The dictatorship of one of
these parties is then no longer in any sense the
dictatorship of the proletariat, but a dictatorship
of one part of the proletariat over the other.   The
situation becomes still more complicated if the
Socialist Parties are divided according to their
relations to non-proletarian elements, and if per-
hance one party attains to power by an alliance of
town proletarians and peasants, then the dictatorship becomes not merely a dictatorship of proletarians over proletarians, but of proletarians and
peasants over proletarians.   The dictatorship of
the proletariat thus assumes a very peculiar form.

What are the grounds for thinking that the
sovereignty of the proletariat must necessarily
take a form which is incompatible with democracy?

Now it may be taken for granted that as a rule
the proletariat will only attain to power when it
represents the majority of the population, or, at
least, has the latter behind it.   Next to its economic
indispensability, the weapon of the proletariat in
its political struggles is its huge numbers.   It may
only expect to carry the day against the resources
of the ruling classes where it has the masses behind
it.   This was the opinion of Marx and Engels, and
therefore they wrote in the Communist Manifesto :
" All previous movements were movements of
minorities, and in the interests of minorities.   The

proletarian movement is the independent movement of the immense majority, in the interest of that majority."

This was true also of the Paris Commune. The first act of the new revolutionary regime was an appeal to the electors. The ballot, taken under conditions of the greatest freedom, gave strong majorities for the Commune in all districts of Paris. Sixty-five revolutionaries were chosen, against 21 of the Opposition, of whom 15 were distinct reactionaries, and six Radical Republicans of the Gambetta school. Among the 65 revolutionaries all the existing phases of French Socialism were represented. However much they fought against each other, no one exercised a dictatorship over the others.

A government so strongly supported by the masses has not the least occasion to interfere with democracy. It cannot dispense with the use of force when this is employed to suppress democracy. Force can only be met by force. But a government which knows that the masses are behind it would only use force to protect democracy, and not to subvert it. It would be committing suicide to cast aside such a strong support as universal suffrage, which is a powerful source of moral authority.

The subversion of democracy by dictatorship

can therefore only be a matter for consideration in exceptional cases, when an extraordinary combination of favourable circumstances enables a proletarian party to take to itself political power, while the majority of the people are either not on its side, or are even against it.

Amongst a people who have been trained in politics for decades, and have run into party moulds, such a chance victory is hardly possible. It is only likely in very backward conditions. If in such a case universal suffrage goes against the Socialist Government, is the latter now to do what we have hitherto demanded of every government, viz., to bow to the will of the people, and to resume its struggle for the power of the State with confidence, on the basis of democracy, or is it to subvert democracy in order to hold on to power?

How can a dictatorship remain at the helm against the will of the majority of the people?

Two ways suggest themselves, that of Jesuitism or that of Bonapartism.

We have already referred to the Jesuit State in Paraguay. The means by which the Jesuits there maintained their authority was their enormous mental superiority to the natives organised by them, who without them were helpless.

Can a Socialist Party acquire such a superiority in a European State? This is quite out of the question. No doubt the proletariat, in the course of the class struggle, raises its mental stature until it is higher than that of other workers, such as peasants, but not without the latter acquiring a political interest and understanding at the same time. The chasm between these various classes is by no means an unbridgable one.

Alongside of the classes of hand workers grows a section of intellectuals, which tends to become more numerous and increasingly necessary for the productive system. Their vocation calls for the acquisition of knowledge and the exercise and development of intelligence.

This section occupies a middle place between the proletariat and the capitalist class. It is not directly interested in capitalism, but is nevertheless mistrustful of the proletariat, so long as it does not consider the latter to be capable of taking its fate into its own hands. Even such members of the cultured classes as most warmly espouse the cause of the freedom of the proletariat stand aloof from the Labour movement in the early stages of the class struggle. They only change their attitude when the proletariat shows increasing capacity in its struggles. The confidence in the proletariat, which is thus inspired in intellectuals who enter the Socialist movement, is not to be confused with the trust which, since August 4,

1914, the Liberal and Centre Parties, and even the Government of Germany, have placed in the Governmental Socialists.

The first kind of confidence is bred by the conviction that the proletariat has acquired the strength and capacity to free itself. The second sort of confidence comes with the conviction that the Socialists in question no longer take the proletariat's fight for freedom seriously.

Without the help, or in opposition to the intellectuals, Socialist production cannot be instituted. In circumstances where the majority of the population mistrust the proletarian party, or stand aloof from it, this attitude would be shared by the bulk of the intellectuals. In that case, a victorious proletarian party would not only be without great intellectual superiority to the rest of the people, but would even be inferior to its opponents in this regard, although its outlook in general social matters might be a much higher one.

The method of Paraguay is therefore not practicable in Europe. There remains to be considered the method adopted by Napoleon the First on Brumaire 18, 1799, and his nephew, the third Napoleon, on December 2, 1852. This consists in governing by the aid of the superiority of a centralised organisation to the unorganised

masses of the people, and the superiority of
military power, arising from the fact that the
armed forces of the Government is opposed to a
people who are defenceless or tired of the armed
struggle.

Can a Socialist system of production be built up
on this foundation? This means the organisation
of production by society, and requires economic
self-government throughout the whole mass of the
people. State organisation of production by a
bureaucracy, or by the dictatorship of a single
section of the people, does not mean Socialism.
Socialism presupposes that broad masses of the
people have been accustomed to organisation, that
numerous economic and political organisations
exist, and can develop in perfect freedom. The
Socialist organisation of Labour is not an affair of
barracks.

A dictatorship of a minority which grants to the
people the fullest freedom of organisation under-
mines its own power by so doing. Should it seek,
on the other hand, to maintain its authority by
restricting this freedom, it impedes development
towards Socialism, instead of furthering it.

A minority dictatorship always finds its most
powerful support in an obedient army, but the
more it substitutes this for majority support, the
more it drives the opposition to seek a remedy by

an appeal to the bayonet, instead of an appeal to
that vote which is denied them. Civil war becomes
the method of adjusting political and social
antagonisms.

Where complete political and social apathy or
dejection does not prevail, the minority dictatorship is always threatened by armed attack, or
constant guerilla warfare, which easily develops
into a protracted armed rising of great masses, to
cope with which all the military power of the
dictatorship is needed.

The dictatorship is then involved in civil war,
and lives in constant danger of being overthrown.

To the building up of a Socialist society there is
no greater obstacle than internal war. In the
present state of extensive geographical division of
labour, the big industries are everywhere closely
dependent on the security of communications no
less than on the security of contract.   External
war would shake the Socialist society to its
foundations, even if the enemy did not penetrate
into the country. Russian Socialists of all sections
in the present Revolution are right in urging the
necessity of peace for the rebuilding of society.

Yet civil war is far more harmful to a Socialist
society than external war, as civil war is fought
out in the land itself, and wastes and paralyses as
much as a foreign invasion.

In the struggles of States it is usually only a question of an accession or loss of power on the part of one or the other government, and not a matter of their very existence. After the war the various belligerent governments and peoples seek to live in peace, if not in amity.

The parties in a civil war are quite differently related to each other. They do not carry on the war to wrest some concessions from the opponents. and then to live with them in peace. And a civil war is also different from democracy, under which minorities are so protected that any party which finds itself in this position, and is obliged to renounce hopes of being the Government, need not relinquish political activity. Every party which is reduced to a minority always retains the right to strive to become the majority, and thereby take over the Government.

In a civil war each party fights for its existence, and the vanquished is menaced with complete destruction. The consciousness of this fact accounts for civil wars being so terrible. A minority which only retains control by military power is inclined to crush its opponents by the bloodiest means, and to decimate them in reckless slaughter, when it is threatened by a revolt, and succeeds in repressing it. June, 1848, in

Paris, and the bloody May week of 1871 have shown this with terrible distinctness.

Chronic civil war, or its alternative under a dictatorship, the apathy and lethargy of the masses, would render the organisation of a Socialist system of production as good as impossible. And yet the dictatorship of the minority, which either produces civil war or apathy, is to be the sovereign means for effecting the transition from Capitalism to Socialism!

Many people confuse civil war with the social revolution, considering this to be its form, and are therefore prepared to excuse the acts of force inevitable in a civil war. This has always been the case in revolutions, they say, and ever will be.

We Social Democrats are decidedly not of the opinion that that which has been must always be. Such ideas of the revolution are formed on the examples of previous middle-class revolutions. The proletarian revolution will be accomplished under quite different conditions from these.

The middle-class revolutions broke out in States in which a despotism, supported by an army separated from the people, suppressed all free movements, in which freedom of the Press, of public meeting, of organisation, and general suffrage did not exist, and in which there was no real representation of the people. There the struggle against the Government necessarily took the form of a civil war. The proletariat of to-day will, as regards Western Europe at least, attain to power in States in which a certain measure of democracy, if not "pure" democracy, has been deeply rooted for decades, and also in which the military are not so cut off from the people as formerly. It remains to be seen how the conquest of political power by the proletariat is achieved under these conditions, where it represents the majority of the people. In no case need we anticipate that in Western Europe the course of the great French Revolution will be repeated. If present-day Russia exhibits so much likeness to the France of 1793, that only shows how near it stands to the stage of middle-class revolution.

The social revolution, the political revolution, and civil war must be distinguished from each other.

The social revolution is a profound transformation of the entire social structure brought about by the establishment of a new method of production. It is a protracted process, which may be spread over decades, and no definite boundaries can be drawn for its conclusion. It will be the more successful, according to the peaceful nature of the forms under which it is consummated. Civil and foreign wars are its deadly foes. As a rule a social revolution is brought about by a political revolution, through a sudden alteration in the relative strength of classes in the State, whereby a class hitherto excluded from the political power possesses itself of the machinery of government. The political revolution is a sudden act, which is rapidly concluded.   Its forms depend on the constitution of the State in which it is accomplished. The more democracy rules, not merely formally, but actually anchored in the strength of the working classes, the greater is the likelihood that the political revolution will be a peaceful one.   Contrariwise, the more the system which has hitherto prevailed has been without the support of a majority of the people, and has represented a minority which kept control by military force, the greater is the likelihood that the political revolution will take the form of a civil war.

Yet, even in the last case, the supporters of the social revolution have a pressing interest in seeing that the civil war is only a transitory episode which quickly terminates, that it is made to serve the sole end of introducing and setting up democracy, to whose pace the social revolution should be adapted.   In other words, the social revolution must not, for the time being, be carried out farther than the majority of the people are inclined to go, because beyond this the Social Revolution, desirable as it may seem to far-seeing individuals, would not find the necessary conditions for establishing itself permanently.

But did not the Reign of Terror of the proletariat and lower middle-class of Paris, that is the dictatorship of a Minority, in the great French Revolution, bring with it enormous consequences of the highest historical significance?

Of course. But of what kind were they? That dictatorship was a child of the war which the allied Monarchs of Europe had waged against Revolutionary France. To have victoriously beaten off this attack was the historical achievement of the Reign of Terror. Thereby is again proved distinctly the old truth, that dictatorship is better able to wage war than democracy. It proves in no way that dictatorship is the method of the proletariat to carry through social transformations to its own liking, and to keep control of political power.

In energy the Reign of Terror of 1793 cannot be surpassed. Yet the proletariat of Paris did not succeed, by this means, in retaining power. The dictatorship was a method by means of which the various fractions belonging to proletarian and small middle-class politics fought amongst themselves, and, finally, it was the means of making an end of all proletarian and lower middle-class politics.

The dictatorship of the lower classes opens the way for the dictatorship of the sword.

Should it be said, after the example of the middle-class revolutions, that the Revolution is synonymous with civil war and dictatorship, then the consequences must also be recognised, and it must be added the Revolution would necessarily end in the rule of a Cromwell or a Napoleon.

This is, however, by no means the necessary upshot of a proletarian revolution where the proletariat forms the majority of the nation, which is democratically organised, and only in such cases do the conditions for Socialist production exist.

By the dictatorship of the proletariat we are unable to understand anything else than its rule on the basis of democracy.

CHAPTER VI.

Constituent Assembly and Soviet.

The contrast between democracy and dictatorship has just acquired an important significance in the Russian Revolution. The Socialists of Russia were from the first divided. They comprised Social Revolutionaries and Marxists. The Social Revolutionaries were, in the first place, the representatives of the peasantry, which in Russia, in contrast to all the rest of Europe, were still a revolutionary factor, and therefore could march with the Socialist proletariat. Against the Social Revolutionaries were the Marxists, the representatives of the industrial proletariat. These divided into two sections, the Mensheviks, who held that only a middle-class revolution was possible in the existing economic conditions in Russia, unless the revolution coincided with a European Socialist revolution, and the Bolsheviks, who always believed in the omnipotence of will and force, and now, without considering the backwardness of Russia, are trying to shape the Revolution on Socialist lines.

In the course of the Revolution the contrast

became more acute.   The Mensheviks considered
it to be their task to take part in a Provisional
Coalition Government until the duly constituted
National Assembly had formed a definite government.   The Bolsheviks endeavoured, even before
the meeting of the National Assembly, to overthrow
this Provisional Government, and replace it by
government of their party.   An additional ground
of opposition came with the question of peace.
The Mensheviks wanted immediate peace as much
as the Bolsheviks, both wanted it on the basis of
Zimmerwald—no   annexations   or   indemnities.
Both sections had been represented at Zimmerwald,
and the Mensheviks had been in the majority there.
But the Mensheviks wanted a general peace, and all
belligerents to adopt the watchword—no annexations or indemnities.   So long as this was not
achieved, the Russian army should keep their arms
in readiness.   The Bolsheviks, on the other hand,
demanded immediate peace at any price, and were
ready, if necessary, to conclude a separate peace,
and they sought to enforce their views by increasing the already great disorganisation of the army.

They were supported by the war weariness of
great masses in the army and among the people, as
well as by the apparent inactivity of the Provisional
Government, which, however, accomplished far
more political and social reform than any other

middle-class government in the same period, although it did not do as much as would be expected of a revolutionary government. The elections for the Constituent Assembly could not be so rapidly completed as was desired. It was first necessary to renew the old official machinery, and to create democratic town and country representation. Enormous difficulties were met with in the compilation of voters' lists in the giant Empire, whose census took place in 1897. So the elections to the Constituent Assembly were constantly postponed.

Above all, peace was no nearer. Wherever the guilt for this may rest, the statesmen of the Entente did not understand how necessary it was for themselves at that time to pronounce in favour of no annexations or indemnities. They pursued a policy which made the Entente appear to the Russian people the obstacle to peace, and with them their Allies the Provisional Government. This was the reason why some of the Mensheviks, the Internationalists, demanded separation from the Entente, and went in opposition to the Provisional Government. Yet they did not go so far as the Bolsheviks. Under these circumstances, the Bolsheviks gained ground at the expense of the Mensheviks and the Provisional Government, which they succeeded in overthrowing in

November, 1917. Their propaganda zeal proved to be so great that they were able to draw a part of the Social Revolutionaries to their side. The left Social Revolutionaries henceforth marched with the Bolsheviks, into whose Government they entered, while the right and also the centre remained on the side of the Mensheviks.

The Bolsheviks drew their strength from the great expectations which they raised. If they were to retain this strength, they had to fulfil these expectations. Was that possible?

The Bolshevist Revolution was based on the supposition that it would be the starting point of a general European Revolution, and that the bold initiative of Russia would summon the proletariat of all Europe to rise.

On these suppositions, it was of no moment what form was taken by the Russian separate peace, what humiliations and burdens it placed on the Russian people, and what interpretations it gave to the principle of the self-determination of peoples. And it was also a matter of indifference whether Russia was capable of defence or not. According to this theory, the European Revolution formed the best defence of the Russian Revolution, for it would bring to the peoples in territory hitherto Russian real and complete self-determination.

The Revolution which would bring about Socialism in Europe would also be the means of removing the obstacles to the carrying through of Socialism in Russia which are created by the economic backwardness of that country.

This was all very logically thought out, and quite well founded, provided the supposition was granted, that the Russian Revolution must inevitably unchain the European Revolution. But what if this did not happen?

The supposition has not yet been realised. And now the proletariat of Europe is blamed for leaving the Russian Revolution in the lurch, and betraying it. This is a complaint against unknown people, for who can be made responsible for the inactivity of the European proletariat.

It is an old Marxist saying that revolutions cannot be made, but arise out of conditions. The conditions of Western Europe are, however, so different from those of Russia that a revolution there would not necessarily provoke one here.

When the Revolution of 1848 broke out in France, it immediately spread over that part of Europe lying east of it. It, however, halted at the Russian boundaries, and when the Revolution was unchained in Russia in 1905, it provoked strong suffrage movements in the countries to the west, although nothing that could be described as a revolution.

But the Bolsheviks must not be too much blamed for expecting a European Revolution. Other Socialists did the same, and we are certainly approaching conditions which will sharply accentuate the class struggle, and which may have many surprises in store. And if the Bolsheviks have up till now been in error in expecting a Revolution, have not Bebel, Marx, and Engels cherished a like delusion? This is not to be denied.

But the latter have never had in mind a revolution at a specific time, and never elaborated their tactics in such wise that the existence of the party and the progress of the class struggle was made to be dependent on the outbreak of the Revolution, so that the proletariat was confronted with the dilemma : revolution or bankruptcy.

Like all politicians they too have erred in their expectations. But such errors have never set them on a false track, and led them into a *cul-de-sac*.

Our Bolshevist comrades have staked all on the card of the general European Revolution. As this card has not turned up, they were forced into a course which brought them up against insoluble problems. They had to defend Russia without an army against powerful and implacable enemies. They had to establish a regime of well-being for all in a state of general dislocation and impoverishment. The less the material and intellectual conditions existed for all that they aspired to, the more they felt obliged to replace what was lacking by the exercise of naked power, by dictatorship. They had to do this all the more the greater the opposition to them amongst the masses became. So it became inevitable that they should put dictatorship in the place of democracy.

If the Bolsheviks were deceived in their expectations that they only needed to become the Government, in order to unchain the European Revolution, they were not less so in the anticipation that they had only to grasp the helm of State, and the majority of the population would joyously range themselves behind them. As the Opposition under the conditions due to Russia's situation, they had indeed developed great propaganda strength, as we have already noted. At the beginning of the Revolution only a small handful, they became so strong eventually as to seize the power of the State. But had they the masses of the population behind them? This should have been revealed by the Constituent Assembly, which the Bolsheviks, like other revolutionaries, had demanded, and for a period even violently demanded; the Constituent

Assembly, to be chosen by universal, equal, direct and secret suffrage.

Immediately after the capture of the Government by the Bolsheviks, the new regime was confirmed by the second All-Russian Congress of Soviets, albeit in opposition to a strong minority, which left the Congress protesting. But even the majority did not yet repudiate the idea of the Constituent Assembly.

The resolution confirming the Soviet Government began with the words : " Pending the calling together of the Constituent Assembly, a Provisional Workers' and Peasants' Government is to be formed, which is to be called the Council of People's Commissaries."

The Constituent Assembly then is recognised here as taking precedence of the Council of People's Commissaries. On November 3 the Government dissolved the Town Council of Petrograd on the ground that it was in conflict with the outlook of the people, as manifested by the Revolution of November 7, and by " the elections to the Constituent Assembly." The new members were proclaimed on the basis of the existing general franchise. Soon, however, a defect was discovered in the elections to the Constituent Assembly.

On December 7, the All-Russian Executive Committee of Soviets published a resolution, in which

it was stated : " However the electoral arrangements of a body composed of elected representatives may be devised, these can only be considered
to be truly democratic and really to represent the
will of the people, when the right of recalling their
members by the electors is recognised and exercised. This principle of real democracy applies to
all representative bodies and also to the Constituent
Assembly. The Congress of the Councils of Workmen's, Soldiers' and Peasants' Delegates, who are
chosen on equal grounds, has the right to issue
writs for a new election in the case of town and
parish councils, and other representative bodies,
not excluding the Constituent Assembly. On the
demand of more than half of the electors of the
circumscription in question the Council must order
a new election."

The demand that the majority of the voters may
at any time recall a deputy, who is no longer in
agreement with their views, is entirely in accordance with the principles of democracy. But it is
not clear, from this standpoint, why the Soviets
should take the step of ordering new elections.
However, at that time this represented the widest
interference with the Constituent Assembly that
had been made. Neither the establishment of the
Assembly, nor the elections were touched.

But it was becoming ever clearer that the

elections had not given the Bolsheviks the majority. Therefore, the *Pravda* of December 26, 1917, published a number of propositions relating to the Constituent Assembly, which Lenin had drawn up, and the Central Committee had accepted. One of them declared that the elections had taken place shortly after the victory of the Bolsheviks, but before the Social Revolutionaries had yet divided. The left and the right Social Revolutionaries had therefore had a common list of candidates. Consequently, the elections gave no clear indication of the real voice of the masses.

Whoever entertained this view, in face of the above-mentioned proposition of December 7, was committed to the conclusion that new elections should be ordered to the Assembly in districts which had chosen social revolutionaries. To what other end had this resolution been drawn up? Yet on December 26 it was already forgotten. And suddenly quite another song was heard in the other proposition of Lenin, with which we are here concerned. After he had shown us that the Assembly just elected was not suitable, because it did not express the real voice of the whole people, he declared that any assembly elected by the masses by general suffrage was not suitable : " The Soviet Republic represents not only a higher form of democratic institutions (in comparison with the middle-class republic and the Constituent Assembly as its consummation) it is also the sole form which renders possible the least painful transition to Socialism.''

It is only a pity that this knowledge was arrived at after one had been left a minority in the Constituent Assembly. Conflict with the Assembly was now inevitable. It ended with a victory for the Soviets, whose dictatorship as a permanent form of government in Russia was proclaimed.

CHAPTER VII.

The Soviet Republic.

The Soviet organisation was a product of the Russian Revolution of 1905. At that time the proletariat engaged in mass action, for which it required a form of mass organisation. The secret organisation of the Social Democrats, as also of the Social Revolutionaries, only comprised hundreds of members who influenced some thousands of workers. Political and industrial mass organisations could not be formed under the Absolutism of the Czar. The only mass organisations of the workers which existed when the Revolution came were those which had been brought into existence by the capitalists themselves and related to single trades. These now became mass organisations for the struggle of the proletariat. Each trade was now transformed from a place where material production was carried on into a place of political propaganda and action. The workers of each trade came together and chose delegates, who united to form a council of delegates, or a Soviet. It was the Mensheviks who gave the impulse to this most significant movement. Thus a form of

proletarian organisation was created, which
became the most comprehensive of all because it
included all wage earners. It has made powerful
action possible, and left a deep impression in the
consciousness of the worker. When the second
Revolution broke out in March, 1917, the Soviet
organisation again came to the fore, and this time
upon a firmer basis, corresponding with the
development undergone by the proletariat since
the first Revolution. The Soviets of 1905 were
local organisations confined to single towns.
Those of 1917 were not only more numerous, but
closely knit together. Single Soviets were affiliated
to a greater body, which in its turn was part of an
organisation comprehending the whole Empire, its
organ being the All-Russian Congress of Soviets,
and a permanent Central Executive Committee.

Already the Soviet organisation can look back
on a great and glorious history. A more important
period lies before it, and not in Russia alone.
Everywhere it is apparent that the usual methods
of the political and economic struggle of the proletariat are not sufficient to cope with the enormous
strength at the disposal of finance capital in the
economic and political spheres.

These methods need not be abandoned, as they
are essential for ordinary conditions, but at times
they are confronted with tasks to which they are

not equal, and success is only likely with a combination of all the economic and political power of the proletariat.

The Russian Revolution of 1905 brought the idea of the mass strike to a head in the German Social Democracy.   This fact was recognised by the 1905 Congress.   That of 1906 endeavoured to allay the sensibilities and fears of the Trade Union officials.   On the question of the mass strike, it resolved that when the executive should consider the necessity for the political mass strike to exist it should get into touch with the General Commission of the Trade Unions, and concert all measures necessary to secure successful action.

After all our experience with the mass strike, we know to-day that this resolution was fundamentally wrong.   For one reason because a mass strike is likely to be all the more successful by breaking out unexpectedly in a particular situation, with spontaneous suddenness.   Its organisation by party and Trade Union machinery would make necessary such preparations as would lead to its frustration.

We, therefore, understand why the Trade Union bureaucracy tends to oppose all spontaneous action on a large scale.   Trade Unions are absolutely necessary.   The proletariat is the stronger the greater the number of its members, and the larger the financial resources of its Trade Unions. Widespread and permanent organisations, with many ramifications, are not possible without a machinery for permanent administration, that is a bureaucracy. The Trade Union bureaucracy is as essential as the Trade Union itself. It has its faults like Parliamentarism and Democracy, but is as indispensable as these for the emancipation of the proletariat.

This is not, however, to say that all its pretentions must be recognised. It should be restricted to its first function, in performing which it cannot be replaced; that is the administration of Trade Union funds, the extension of organisation, and the giving advice to the workers in their struggles. But it is unsuitable for leading that powerful mass strike which tends to become the characteristic of the times.

By virtue of their experience and knowledge, Trade Union officials and Parliamentarians may here successfully assist, but the initiative tends to fall into the hands of Workshop Committees. In various countries outside Russia, such as in England, these institutions (shop stewards) have played a big part in mass struggles, side by side with ordinary Trade Unionism.

The Soviet organisation is, therefore, one of the most important phenomena of our time. It promises to acquire an outstanding significance in the great decisive struggles between Capital and Labour which are before us.

Can we ask even more than this of the Soviets? The Bolshevists, who, together with the left-wing Social Revolutionaries, obtained a majority in the Russian Workers' Councils after the November Revolution of 1917, after the dissolution of the Constituent Assembly, proceeded to make an organ of government of the Soviets, which hitherto had been the fighting organisation of a class. They did away with the democratic institutions which had been conquered by the Russian people in the March Revolution. Quite properly the Bolsheviks ceased to call themselves Social Democrats, and described themselves as Communists.

Indeed, they did not repudiate democracy entirely. In his speech of April 28, Lenin described the Soviet organisation as a higher type of democracy, a complete break with its "middle-class distortion." Entire freedom was now secured to the proletarian and the poor peasant.

Hitherto democracy had connoted equal political rights for all citizens. The sections privileged by law had always possessed freedom of movement. But one does not call that democracy. The Soviet Republic is to be the organ of the dictatorship of the proletariat, the only means, as

Lenin expresses it, whereby the most painless transition to Socialism is made possible. This is to be done by depriving of political rights all those who are not represented in the Soviets.

Why should this step make less painful the transition to Socialism than would be the case with universal suffrage? Obviously, because the capitalists are in this way excluded from the making of laws.

Now there are two alternatives. Suppose the capitalists and their supporters are an insignificant handful. How could they then prevent the transition to Socialism under universal suffrage? On the contrary, universal suffrage would reveal them as an insignificant minority, and consequently they would the sooner resign themselves to their fate than if the franchise were so shaped that no-one could say with certainty which party had behind it a majority of the people. In reality, however, the capitalists cannot be deprived of rights. What is a capitalist in a legal sense? A possessor.

Even in a country so highly developed economically as Germany, where the proletariat is so numerous, the establishment of a Soviet Republic would disfranchise great masses of the people. In 1907, the number of men, with their families, belonging to occupations which comprised the three great groups of agriculture, industry and trade, that is, wage-earners and salaried persons, amounted to something over 35,000,000, as against 17,000,000 belonging to other sections. A party could therefore very well have the majority of wage-earners behind it and yet form a minority of the population. On the other hand, when the workers vote together, they need not fear the united votes of their opponents. By obliging them to fight their common foes, universal suffrage causes them to close up their ranks sooner than if the political struggle were confined to the Soviets, from which the opponents are excluded, and in which the political struggle of a Socialist party takes the form of attacking another Socialist Party. Instead of class-consciousness, sectarian fanaticism is thereby induced.

Now for the other alternative. Suppose the capitalists and their supporters are not a small minority. but a great mass which is well able, in a Parliament elected on the basis of universal suffrage, to constitute a respectable opposition?

What purpose would be served by reducing this opposition to silence in the governing body? The capitalists themselves are everywhere only a small section. But in comparison with the Socialists, their supporters may be very numerous. It should not be thought that only personal interest

or payment would induce people to enter the lists
for capitalism.   Except Socialism, capitalism is
to-day the only possible method of production on a
large scale.

Who holds Socialism to be impossible, must, if
he thinks in a modern sense at all, be for
capitalism, even if he be not interested therein.
Even of those backward sections, who are opposed
to capitalism, many take their stand on the basis
of private property in the means of production,
and therefore on the basis on which capitalism
grows.   In a backward country, therefore, the
number of those in the population who directly or
indirectly would protect capitalism may be very
large.   Their opposition would not be lessened if
they were deprived of political rights.   They would
all the more energetically oppose the measures of
the new tyrannical regime.   By universal suffrage
in a real democracy all classes and interests are
represented in the governing body according to
their strength.   Every section and party may
exercise the fullest criticism upon each Bill, show
up all its weaknesses, and also make known the
strength of the opposition which exists amongst
the people.   In the Soviet all hostile criticism is
excluded, and the weaknesses of laws do not come
so easily to light.   The opposition which they
arouse amongst the population is not learned in
the first instance.

Only afterwards, when the law is promulgated, do criticism and opposition manifest themselves. Instead of during the debates, the weaknesses of laws come to light when they are put into operation. Even the Soviet Government has already, in the case of very important laws, been obliged, by supplements and lax administration, to let in by the backdoor elements that it solemnly threw out of the front door.

That, as compared with general suffrage, vote by occupation has a tendency to narrow the outlook of the electors, we have already shown. That by this means the transition to Socialism is rendered painless is very much in doubt.

Not less doubtful is the dictatorship of the proletariat under the Soviet regime. Dictatorship, certainly. But of the proletariat?

In the economic structure of Russia the Soviets could only attain the position of rulers in 1917 by not confining themselves to the industrial proletariat of the towns, as in 1905. This time the soldiers and peasants were also organised in Soviets. With the disbanding of the army the soldiers have lost their numerical importance. The small army raised by the People's Commissaries was more useful to them, from the point of view of bayonets than of votes. Nevertheless, the votes of the Red Army have played a considerable part. In some Soviets, for example, at the latest elections in Petrograd the major portion of the mandates were reserved to its members. Of much more importance, however, were the votes of the peasants, who comprise the great majority of the Russian people. What is represented to us as the dictatorship of the proletariat, if it were logically carried out and a class were able to exercise directly the dictatorship which is only possible for a party, would turn out to be the dictatorship of the peasants. It would therefore appear that the least painful transition to Socialism is effected when it is carried out by the peasants. Although the peasants form the majority in the Soviet organisations, these do not include the whole of the proletariat.

At first it was not clear who might organise in Soviets, and which Soviets might affiliate to the general organisation. It was thought by various people that every trade organisation might form a Soviet, and be regarded as such.

On May 28, 1918, the *Leipziger Volkszeitung* published an article entitled the Soviet Republic, which obviously came from Bolshevist sources. It was there stated :

" The Soviet representation is superior to democratic representation. It concedes to all citizens full and equal rights, and all classes in the

land enjoy the full possibility of securing representation in the Soviets, exactly corresponding to
their strength and special social importance.   To
this end they must be independently organised,
not in parties, as hitherto, on the lines of democracy, but in special classes or trade organisations."

Legien and his friends may be very contented
with this subordination of the Social Democratic
Party to the Trade Unions, as well as the reactionaries who want to substitute a class vote for
general suffrage.   The champion of proletarian
dictatorship continues :

" The middle classes as such have hitherto not
been represented in the Soviets, because on the
one hand, they have boycotted them, and on the
other, are not disposed to be organised on the proletarian scheme, but not because they have been
excluded."

Are they really not so disposed?   Has our
Bolshevist friend ever belonged to an employers'
association, and does he think that the capitalist
isolated under general suffrage is really more
dangerous than an employers' association in a
Soviet?

But we are about to learn wherein consists the
superiority of the Soviet organisation over general
suffrage : " It can obviously adopt the attitude of

excluding any middle-class organisation from the Soviets."

In other words, the Soviet organisation has the advantage over general suffrage of being more arbitrary.   It can exclude all organisations which it considers obnoxious.   It "concedes full and equal rights to citizens," but "obviously" they must only be exercised to the liking of the Soviet Government.

Meanwhile, it has been discovered that this does not work.   The last All-Russian Congress of Soviets, which terminated on July 12, 1918, drafted a constitution of the Russian Soviet Republic.   This lays it down that not all the inhabitants of the Russian Empire, but only specified categories have the right to elect deputies to the Soviets.   All those may vote "who procure their sustenance by useful or productive work." What is "useful and productive work"?   This is a very elastic term.   Not less elastic is the definition of those who are excluded from the franchise. They include any who employ wage labourers for profit.   A home worker or small master, with an apprentice, may live and feel quite like a proletarian, but he has no vote.   Even more proletarians may become disfranchised by the definition which aims at depriving private traders and middle men of the vote.   The worker who loses his work, and endeavours to get a living by opening a small shop, or selling newspapers, loses his vote.

Another clause excludes from the franchise everyone who has unearned income, for example, dividends on capital, profits of a business, rent of property. How big the unearned income must be which carries with it loss of the vote is not stated. Does it include the possession of a savings bankbook? Quite a number of workers, especially in the small towns, own a little house, and, to keep themselves above water, let lodgings. Does this bring them into the category of people with unearned income. Not long since there was a strike at the Obuchovist Factory, "this hotbed of the Revolution," as Trotsky styled it in 1909 (Russia in the Revolution, page 83). I asked a Bolshevist comrade how he explained this protest against the Soviet Government.

"That is very simple," he said, "the workers there are all capitalists who own a little house."

One sees how little it takes, according to the Constitution of the Soviet Republic, to be labelled a capitalist, and to lose the vote.

The elasticity of the definition of the franchise, which opens the door to the greatest arbitrariness, is due to the subject of this definition, and not to its framers. A juridical definition of the proletariat, which shall be distinct and precise, is not to be had.

I have not found a reference to the appointment of a specific authority which shall verify each person's vote, compile voting lists, and carry out the election, either by secret ballot or a show of hands. Clause 70 determines: "The exact procedure of election will be decided by the local Soviets, in accordance with instructions from the All-Russian Central Committee."

In a speech of April 28, 1918, Lenin mentioned the following in connection with the Socialist character of the Soviets: (1) The voters are the working and exploited masses, only the middle classes being excluded; (2) All bureaucratic formality and restriction cease. The masses themselves decide the procedure and the date of the elections.

It seems, then, that any body of electors may order the electoral procedure according to their whims. This would give the greatest scope for arbitrary action, and make it possible to get rid of any inconvenient element of opposition within the proletariat itself.

It need only be remarked in passing that the election to the regional Soviet is an indirect one, which in any case makes easy the influencing of elections to the detriment of the opposition.

However, this has not prevented the opposition from coming to expression in the Soviets.

The "least painful transition" to Socialism obviously requires the silencing of all opposition and criticism. So on June 14, 1918, the All-Russian Central Committee passed this resolution :

" The representatives of the Social Revolutionary Party (the right wing and the centre) are excluded, and at the same time all Soviets of Workers', Soldiers', Peasants' and Cossacks' Deputies are recommended to expel from their midst all representatives of this fraction."

This measure was not directed against particular persons, who had committed some punishable acts. Anyone offending in this way against the existing order would at once be imprisoned, and there would be no need to exclude him. There is no word in the constitution of the Soviet Republic respecting the immunity of deputies. Not particular persons (but particular parties were thereby excluded from the Soviets. This means in practice nothing less than that all proletarians, who take their stand on the ground of party, lose their votes. Their votes are no longer counted. For this no specific clause exists. Clause 23 of the Constitution of the Soviet Republic determines : " In the interests of the working class as a whole the Russian Socialist Federal Soviet Republic may withdraw rights from any persons or groups who misuse them to the detriment of the Socialist Revolution."

This declared the whole opposition to be out-laws. For every Government, even a revolution-ary one, discovers that the opposition misuse their rights. Yet even this was not sufficient to ensure the painless transition to Socialism.

Scarcely had the Bolsheviks got rid of the opposition of the Mensheviks and the Centre and Right Wing of the Social Revolutionaries within the Soviets, when the great fight broke out between them and the left Social Revolutionaries, with whom they had formed the government. The greater part of these were now driven out of the Soviets.

So within the proletariat itself the circle of those who participate in political rights, upon whom the Bolshevist regime rests, becomes ever smaller. Starting out with the idea of establish-ing the dictatorship of the proletariat the Bolshevist regime was bound to become the dictatorship of a party within the proletariat. Yet it might be for a long time the dictatorship of the majority of the proletariat over the minority. To-day even that has become doubtful.

Nevertheless, every regime, even a dictator-ship, is under the necessity of appearing to be the expression of the needs of the majority, not merely of the proletariat, but of the whole people. Even the Bolsheviks cannot escape from this.

The *Populaire* of Paris, on July 6, 1918, reported an interview which Longuet had with Litvinoff, the London Bolshevik Ambassador. Among other things Longuet remarked :

"You know, citizen Litvinoff, that even the comrades in the West, who have the strongest sympathy for your movement, are pained by the dissolution of the Constituent Assembly. I had already told you this on my own account, when I last saw you in January. Do you not think that, in order to meet the attacks that are made on you, you ought at any rate to hold new elections?"

To which Litvinoff replied :

"This is not possible at the moment in view of the present situation. Democracy expressed in the form of the Soviets—a more precise expression of the will of the masses—is the sole form of representation suitable to Russia at the present time. Besides those who protested against the last Soviet elections, which were disastrous for them, would also oppose elections for a new Assembly, in which we should certainly have the majority."

If Comrade Litvinoff and his friends are so sure of this, why do not they take steps to hold such elections. If these were held in the fullest freedom, and gave a Bolshevist majority, the existing Government would gain a far stronger moral basis

at home and abroad than ever it can win as a
Soviet Government on the present methods of
election and administration. Above all, Socialist
critics would lose every ground of objection, and
the whole International of the fighting proletariat
would stand behind them with unanimity and
with full force.

Why renounce this enormous advantage if one is
so sure of a majority?   Because general suffrage
is not suitable to Russia at the present time, and
only the Soviet organisation meets its requirements? But how can this assertion be proved? It
is indeed understandable when one remembers
that every Government likes to identify itself with
the country, and to declare that what does not suit
it is also not suitable for the country.

One thing can certainly be granted.   The
present situation is not favourable to the suggestion of elections to a Constituent Assembly.   At
the time when the elections to the first Assembly
were prepared and completed a certain amount of
peace still prevailed in the interior.   To-day all
Russia is torn by civil war.   Does, however, this
record of nine months of the Soviet Republic furnish the proof that the Soviet organisation is the
most suitable to Russia, and the one which least
painfully effects the transition to Socialism?

CHAPTER VIII.

THE OBJECT LESSON.

THE pernicious features of the method of dictatorship here discussed must now be contrasted with more favourable aspects. It furnishes a striking object lesson, and even if it cannot last it is able to accomplish many things to the advantage of the proletariat, which cannot be lost.

Let us look closely at the object lesson. This argument obviously rests on the following consideration : Under democracy, by virtue of which the majority of the people rule, Socialism can only be brought about when a majority in its favour, is gained. A long and tedious way. We reach our goal far quicker if an energetic minority which knows its aims, seizes hold of the power of the State, and uses it for passing Socialist measures. Its success would at once compel conviction, and the majority, which hitherto had opposed, would quickly rally to Socialism.

This sounds very plausible, and sounded so in the mouth of old Weitling. It has only the one defect that it assumes that which has to be proved.

The opponents of the method of dictatorship contest the assumption that Socialist production can be brought about by a minority without the co-operation of the great mass of the people. If the attempt fails, it certainly is an object lesson, but in the wrong sense, not by attracting, but by frightening.

People who are influenced by such an object lesson, and not by examining and verifying social relations, thoughtless worshippers of mere success, would, in the case of the attempt failing, not inquire from what causes it did not succeed. They would not seek for the explanation in the unfavourable or unripe conditions, but in Socialism itself, and would conclude that Socialism is realisable under no circumstances.

It is apparent that the object lesson has a very dangerous side.

How has it been represented to us?

We may popularly express the essentials of Socialism in the words : Freedom and bread for all. This is what the masses expect from it, and why they rally to it. Freedom is not less important than bread. Even well-to-do and rich classes have fought for their freedom, and not seldom have made the biggest sacrifices for their convictions in blood and treasure. The need for freedom, for self-determination, is as natural as the need for food.

Hitherto Social Democracy did represent to the masses of the people the object lesson of being the most tireless champion of the freedom of all who were oppressed, not merely the wage-earner, but also of women, persecuted religions and races, the Jews, Negroes and Chinese. By this object lesson it has won adherents quite outside the circle of wage-earners.

Now, so soon as Social Democracy attains to power, this object lesson is to be replaced by one of an opposite character. The first step consists in the suspension of universal suffrage and of liberty of the Press, the disfranchisement of large masses of the people, for this must always take place if dictatorship is substituted for democracy. In order to break the political influence of the upper ten thousand, it is not necessary to exclude them from the franchise. They exercise this influence not by their personal votes. As regards small shopkeepers, home workers, peasants who are well off and in moderate condition, the greater part of the intellectuals, so soon as the dictatorship deprives them of their rights, they are changed at once into enemies of Socialism by this kind of object lesson, so far as they are not inimical from the beginning. Thus all those who adhere to Socialism on the ground that it fights for the freedom of all would become enemies of the proletarian dictatorship.

This method will win nobody who is not already a Socialist.   It can only increase the enemies of Socialism.

But we saw that Socialism not only promised freedom, but also bread.   This ought to reconcile those whom the Communist dictatorship robbed of freedom.

They are not the best of the masses who are consoled in their loss of freedom with bread and pleasure.   But without doubt material well-being will lead many to Communism who regard it sceptically, or who are by it deprived of their rights. Only this prosperity must really come, and that quickly, not as a promise for the future, if the object lesson is to be effective.

How is this prosperity to be attained? The necessity for dictatorship pre-supposes that a minority of the population have possessed themselves of the power of the State. A minority composed of those who possess nothing. The greatest weapon of the proletariat is, however, its numbers, and in normal times it can only progress on these lines, conquering the political power only when it forms the majority.   As a minority it can only achieve power by the combination of extraordinary circumstances, by a catastrophe which causes the collapse of a regime, and leaves the State helpless and impoverished.

Under such circumstances, Socialism, that is general well-being within modern civilisation, would only be possible through a powerful development of the productive forces which capitalism brings into existence, and with the aid of the enormous riches which it creates and concentrates in the hands of the capitalist class. A State which by a foolish policy or by unsuccessful war has dissipated these riches, is by its nature condemned to be an unfavourable starting point for the rapid diffusion of prosperity in all classes.

If, as the heir of the bankrupt State, not a democratic but a dictatorial regime enters into power, it even renders the position worse, as civil war is its necessary consequence. What might still be left in the shape of material resources is wasted by anarchy.

In fine, the uninterrupted progress of production is essential for the prosperity of all. The destruction of capitalism is not Socialism. Where capitalist production cannot be transformed at once into Socialist production, it must go on as before, otherwise the process of production will be interrupted, and that hardship for the masses will ensue which the modern proletariat so much fears in the shape of general unemployment.

In those places where, under the new conditions, capitalist production has been rendered impossible, Socialist production will only be able to replace it if the proletariat has acquired experience in self-government, in trade unions, and on town councils, and has participated in the making of laws and the control of government, and if numerous intellectuals are prepared to assist with their services the new methods.

In a country which is so little developed economically that the proletariat only forms a minority, such maturity of the proletariat is not to be expected.

It may therefore be taken for granted that in all places where the proletariat can only maintain itself in power by a dictatorship, instead of by democracy, the difficulties with which Socialism is confronted are so great that it would seem to be out of the question that dictatorship could rapidly bring about prosperity for all, and in this manner reconcile to the reign of force the masses of the people who are thereby deprived of political rights.

As a matter of fact, we see that the Soviet Republic, after nine months of existence, instead of diffusing general prosperity, is obliged to explain how the general poverty arises.

We have lying before us : " Theses respecting the Socialist Revolution and the tasks of the proletariat during its dictatorship in Russia," which emanates from the Bolshevist side. A passage deals with " the difficulties of the position."

Paragraph 28 reads as follows : " 28. The proletariat has carried out positive organic work under the greatest difficulties. The internal difficulties are : The wearing out and enormous exhaustion of the social resources and even their dissolution in consequence of the war, the policy of the capitalist class before the October revolution (their calculated policy of disorganisation, in order, after the ' Anarchy,' to create a middle-class dictatorship), the general sabotage of the middle-class and the intellectuals after the October revolution ; the permanent counter-revolutionary revolt of the ex-officers, generals and middle classes, with arms or without ; *lack of technical skill and experience on the part of the working-class itself* (italicised in original), lack of organising experience ; the existence of large masses of the small middle class, which are an unorganised class, par excellence, etc."

This is all very true. But it does not indicate anything else than that the conditions are not ripe. And does it not strikingly show that an object lesson

on the lines of Socialism is, under these conditions
in present-day Russia, not to be thought of? It is
a famous object lesson which makes it necessary for
theoretical arguments to be set out why that
which is to be shown is not possible at the moment.
Will it convert those who have hitherto opposed
Socialism, and who are only to be convinced by
its practical success?

Of course, a new regime will come up against
unexpected difficulties. It is wrong to lay the
blame for them on this regime, as a matter of
course, and to be discouraged by them without
closer examination of the circumstances. But if
one is to persevere, in spite of these difficulties,
then it is necessary to win beforehand a strong
conviction of the justice and necessity of this
regime. Only then will confusion be avoided.
Success worshippers are always uncertain Can-
tonists.

So we are driven back upon democracy, which
obliges us to strive to enlighten and convince the
masses by intensive propaganda before we can
reach the point of bringing Socialism about. We
must here again repudiate the method of dictatorship, which substitutes compulsory object lessons
for conviction.

This is not to say that object lessons may avail
nothing in the realisation of Socialism. On the

contrary, they can and will play a great part in this, but not through the medium of dictatorship.

The various States of the world are at very different stages of economic and political development. The more a State is capitalistic on the one side and democratic on the other, the nearer it is to Socialism. The more its capitalist industry is developed, the higher is its productive power, the greater its riches, the more socially organised its labour, the more numerous its proletariat; and the more democratic a State is, the better trained and organised is its proletariat. Democracy may sometimes repress its revolutionary thought, but it is the indispensable means for the proletariat to attain that ripeness which it needs for the conquest of political power, and the bringing about of the social revolution. In no country is a conflict between the proletariat and the ruling classes absent, but the more a country is progressive in capitalism and democracy, the greater is the prospect of the proletariat, in such a conflict, of not merely gaining a passing victory, but also of maintaining it.

Where a proletariat, under such conditions, gains control of the State, it will discover sufficient material and intellectual resources to permit it at once to give the economic development a Socialist direction, and immediately to increase the general well-being.

This will then furnish a genuine object lesson to
countries which are economically and politically
backward. The mass of their proletariat will now
unanimously demand measures on the same lines,
and also all other sections of the poorer classes, as
well as numerous intellectuals, will demand that
the State should take the same road to general
prosperity. Thus, by the example of the progressive countries, the cause of Socialism will
become irresistible in countries which to-day are
not so advanced as to allow their proletariat of its
own strength to conquer the power of the State,
and put Socialism into operation.

And we need not place this period in the distant
future. In a number of industrial States the
material and moral prerequisites for Socialism
appear already to exist in sufficient measure. The
question of the political dominion of the proletariat is merely a question of power alone, above
all of the determination of the proletariat to engage
in resolute class struggle. But Russia is not one of
these leading industrial States. What is being
enacted there now is, in fact, the last of middle
class, and not the first of Socialist revolutions.
This shows itself ever more distinctly. Its present
Levolution could only assume a Socialist character
if it coincided with Socialist Revolutions in Western
Europe.

That by an object lesson of this kind in the more highly-developed nations, the pace of social development may be accelerated, was already recognised by Marx in the preface to the first edition of " Capital " :

" One nation can and should learn from others. And even when a society has got upon the right track for the discovery of the natural laws of its movement—it can neither clear by bold leaps, nor remove by legal enactments the obstacles offered by the successive phases of its normal development. But it can shorten and lessen the birth-pangs."

In spite of their numerous calls on Marx, our Bolshevist friends seem to have quite forgotten this passage, for the dictatorship of the proletariat, which they preach and practise, is nothing but a grandiose attempt to clear by bold leaps or remove by legal enactments the obstacles offered by the successive phases of normal development.   They think that it is the least painful method for the delivery of Socialism, for " shortening and lessening its birth-pangs."   But if we are to continue in metaphor, then their practice reminds us more of a pregnant woman, who performs the most foolish exercises in order to shorten the period of gestation, which makes her impatient, and thereby causes a premature birth.

The result of such proceedings is, as a rule, a child incapable of life.

Marx speaks here of the object lesson which one nation may afford another. Socialism is, however, concerned with yet another kind of object lesson, viz., that which a highly-developed industry may furnish to an industry which is backward.

To be sure, capitalist competition everywhere tends to displace old-fashioned industrial methods, but under capitalist conditions this is so painful a process that those threatened by its operation strive to avert it by all means. The Socialist method of production would therefore find in existence a number of processes which are technically obsolete; for example, in agriculture, where large-scale production has made little progress, and in places is even receding.

Socialist production can only develop on the basis of the large industry. Socialist agriculture would have to consist solely in the socialisation of what large-scale production already exists. If good results are thereby obtained, which is to be expected, provided the social labour of freely-organised men is substituted for wage labour, (which only produces very inadequate results in agriculture) the conditions of the workers in the large Socialist industry will be seen to be more favourable than those of the small peasants, and it may then be anticipated with certainty that the latter will voluntarily pass over to the new productive methods, when society furnishes them with the necessary means. But not before. In agriculture the way for Socialism is not prepared by Capitalism in any adequate measure. And it is quite hopeless to try to convince peasant proprietors of the theoretical superiority of Socialism. Only the object lesson of the socialisation of peasant agriculture can help. This, however, presupposes a certain extension of large-scale agriculture. The object lesson will be the quicker and more effective according to the degree of development of large-scale industry in the country.

The policy of the lower middle class democrats, which has been taken up by Social Democrats of the David school, and in some respects made more extreme, that is, the destruction of any large-scale agriculture and its partition into small-scale industry, is sharply opposed to Socialism as applied to agriculture, and therefore to Socialism as applied to society generally.

The most striking feature of the present Russian Revolution is its working out on the lines of Eduard David. He, and not Lenin, has given the Revolution its peculiar direction in this respect. That is the Socialist instruction which it imparts. It testifies, in fact, to its middle-class character.

CHAPTER IX.

The Legacy of the Dictatorship.
(a) Agriculture.

Dictatorship is not only going to furnish the best object lesson for Socialist propaganda, but will also hasten progress towards Socialism, by its actions, in the event of its not maintaining itself and collapsing before the goal has been reached. Its supporters expect that it will leave behind much that cannot be set on one side, and that it has cleared out of the way much that cannot be again established.

This conception, too, like so many others, is based on the observation of the great French Revolution, the middle-class revolution, under the influence of which remain those who stigmatise as "middle class," and reject, all that does not suit them, and for whom democracy is only a middle-class prejudice.

The observation is correct, but the conclusions to be drawn are other than those of the supporters of dictatorship. The latter may be able to achieve more radical things than democracy, but what accompanies it is not always what the dictators want. However high the dictatorship may be raised above all other powers in the State, it is always dependent upon one of them : that is the material foundations of society. These conditions, and not the will of the dictators, decide what the final consequences of the dictatorship will be.

The strongest driving force of the Reign of Terror in the French Revolution was the proletariat and the semi-proletarian classes of Paris. What they desired was the equalisation of all property, the destruction of large properties. This they succeeded in doing in various ways. But they destroyed only more thoroughly than has happened in other parts of Europe the vestiges of feudalism, and thereby more effectively opened the way for the coming of the new capitalist large property, which shot up like a fungus immediately after the downfall of the Reign of Terror. That, and in nowise economic equality, was the legacy of that dictatorship of the equalitarians.

In order to understand what the economic legacy of the present dictatorship of the Soviets will be, we must not only take account of their intentions, desires and measures, but of the economic structure of the Empire. It is decisive.

This examination may appear to many as tedious pedantry, incompatible with the revolutionary fire which burned in a Marx. No one can say with certainty what Marx would have thought and done

in the present situation. But it is certain that this
tedious pedantry is the only procedure which is
compatible with historical materialism, the foundation of which is one of the indisputable merits of
Marx. A man who believed that in a question of
knowledge mere enthusiasm was to be accounted
higher than experience would have been pushed on
one side by Marx as an empty phrasemonger.

The economic foundation of present-day Russia
is still agriculture, and even small peasant agriculture. By it live four-fifths, perhaps even five-
sixths of its inhabitants.   In the year 1913 the
town population of Russia (excluding Finland) was
computed at 24 millions, and those living by the
land were 147 millions. The overwhelming majority
of the latter are peasants. The Revolution has
altered nothing in these conditions.   During the
past year they have even been strengthened.
Numerous workers have returned to the land. In
the towns hunger has been more devastating than
amongst the peasants.

Until the Revolution the peasants lived under a
semi-feudal yoke. Serfage had indeed been
abolished by the Reform of 1861, and the peasant
formally made a free man.   But this was not the
work of a revolution, but the work of a patriarchal
absolutism, which in a fatherly spirit provided that
the big landowners should lose nothing by the

Reform, but should rather gain. The peasant had
to pay for his freedom with the loss of a part of the
land which, prior to the Reform, he had used, and
had to pay dear for the land which would be
granted to him. The average size of a peasant's
holding was certainly larger than in Western
Europe. Before the Revolution the peasants'
holdings of less than five hectares in Russia comprised only 10.6 per cent. of the total, whereas in
France 71.4 per cent. of the holdings were five
hectares and less, and in Germany 76.5 per cent.
But Russian agriculture is so backward through
the ignorance of the peasants, primitive appliances, lack of cattle and manure, that it produces
far less than in Western Europe. In France 70.5
pud of wheat (1 pud = 16.38 kilogrammes) is
raised from every hectare, in Germany 77 pud, but
in Russia only 28.2 pud. (Massloff : the Russian
Agrarian Question.)

The peasant was therefore soon after his emancipation in a worse material position than before.
He became impoverished, and his industry did not
progress, but rather declined. To avoid star-
vation, he was obliged to rent plots of land from
the large land-owners, or, where these were themselves engaged in large-scale agriculture, to work
for wages. Mostly, he was obliged to obtain an
advance for the work he was to do, which brought

him into a state of indebtedness that was often more oppressive and hopeless than his former serfdom. This state of affairs was not improved by the peasant taking his produce to the markets, whether home or foreign. This put money in his pocket, and made it possible for him to save, which could, however, only be done at the cost of the peasant's sustenance. Formerly, he had consumed the greater part of his produce himself, because he had no other outlet. Now that he found an outlet, he sold as much as possible, and kept as little as possible back. So every year of failure became a year of hunger. So far as the peasant could save money, he did not spend it to improve his methods, but to obtain more land.

In the period between 1863 and 1892, agricultural land in European Russia was

	Million Roubles.	
	Bought.	Sold.
By nobles	821 ...	1,459
By merchants	318 ...	135
By peasants	335 ...	93

The land of the nobles decreased, and that of the peasants increased as compared with the middle class of the towns. But the land population increased more rapidly still, and so on the average there was a decrease in the area belonging to each peasant, although the total holdings of the peasants slightly increased.   At the same time, under the influence of money transactions, aided by the legislature, the village communism, which from time to time had been instrumental in equalising the land holdings of individual peasants, disappeared more and more.   Individuals were prosperous, but the others were the more impoverished.   Both, however, prosperous and poor peasants, looked ever more greedily to the great land-owners, from whom they expected their salvation.   They longed for the overthrow of landed property, and became a revolutionary class.   Their longing found expression and form through the revolutionary intellectuals of the towns.   The Socialists of Russia were agreed that a revolution in the ownership of land was as essential for Russia as the overthrow of the Czarist absolutism.   But the Socialists were divided into two sections.   The one believed that primitive village communism would enable the peasants, and with them all Russia, to attain to Socialism at one bound, although it may be a Socialism of their own.   This shade of opinion found various expressions, the chief being the Social Revolutionaries. The Marxists opposed them on the ground that Russia, as little as other countries, " could clear by leaps or remove by legal enactments the obstacles offered by the successive phases of normal development,'' that the coming Revolution could only clear away the vestiges of Feudalism, and accelerate the capitalist development, on the basis of which would grow up a proletariat trained by the newly-won democracy, which, then, being on the same level as the proletariat of Western Europe, would be able to achieve Socialism at the same time as the latter.

All Socialists without distinction were agreed in supporting the peasants in their endeavours to remove the vestiges of Feudalism. This was distinctly brought to the mind of the peasant in the Revolution of 1905. From then onwards the co-operation of peasants and Socialists, namely, through the means of the Social Revolutionaries, assumed a closer character. Thus after the Revolution of 1917 the organisation of the Soviets arose as not merely a proletarian, but also a peasant institution.

The Revolution made possession of large estates untenable. This became obvious at once. It was inevitable that they should be transferred to the peasant population, although there was by no means agreement as to the methods of carrying this out. Various solutions were conceivable. From the Socialist standpoint, the most rational would have been to transform the large estates into State property, and have them worked on a co-operative basis by the peasants, who had hitherto been engaged on them as wage-earners. However, this solution presupposed an agricultural class which Russia did not possess.   Another solution would have been for the big landed estates to become State property, and to be divided into small parcels to be rented to the peasants who needed land.   Even that would have been a partial realisation of Socialism.   But the small peasant holders strove where they could to obtain full private property in their means of production. This character they have hitherto displayed everywhere, and the Russian peasant, in spite of the tradition of village communism, is no exception. The breaking up of landed estates and their partition—that was his programme, and he was strong enough to carry it out.   No one could hinder him. In the interests of the peasants themselves, it would have been nevertheless very desirable that the partition should be systematically carried out, and the land given to those who needed it the most, and could also use it.   There was only one authority which could have effected such a systematic partition, and that was the Constituent Assembly, as representing the collective will of the nation, of whom the great majority were peasants.

But this was too long to wait.   The peasants

began everywhere to help themselves, which caused many valuable productive implements to be destroyed. The Soviet Organisation then removed from the purview of the Constituent Assembly the settlement of the Agrarian question, and left it to the peasants of every commune to seize the big estates, and proceed with their partition according to their whim. One of the first resolutions of the Soviet Government ordered that

(1) Private property in land is forthwith abolished, without compensation.

(2) The property of the landlords, together with the appurtenances, cloisters, and church property, with all live-stock and chattels, and other belongings, pending the decision of the land question by the Constituent Assembly, shall be placed at the disposal of the Local Committees and the Councils of Peasants' Deputies.

The reference to the Constituent Assembly remained a dead letter. In practice the peasants of the localities took what they wanted of the estates.

This necessarily excluded any equalisation between rich localities, containing many substantial peasants, and poor neighbourhoods containing none but small peasants. Within the individual communes no record was made of those who obtained the land.   Where the rich peasants dominated, either by their numbers or their influence, they obtained the lion share of the big estates.   No general statistics regarding the partition of the land were compiled, but it was frequently stated that, as a rule, the big peasants came away with most of the land that was partitioned.

It is certain that the Soviet Republic has not solved the Agrarian question on the lines of an equitable division of the land.   At the beginning the peasant Soviets constituted an organisation of the peasants alone.   To-day it is announced that the Soviets represent the organisation of the proletariat and the poor peasants.   The well-to-do have lost their right of voting in the Soviets.   The poor peasant is here recognised as the colossal and permanent product of the Socialist agrarian reform of the dictatorship of the proletariat.   This peasant is very likely in the minority in many villages, otherwise there was no object in protecting him by disfranchising the prosperous and medium peasants.   But in any case he still forms a very considerable fraction of the Russian peasantry.

By this partition of property the Soviet Republic sought to appease the peasants.   It would have been dangerous for it to interfere even slightly with peasant private property.

To be sure it encroached on the relations between rich and poor peasants, but not by a fresh partition of the land. To remedy the lack of food in the towns detachments of armed workers were sent into the villages, to take away from the rich peasants their surplus food. Part of this was assigned to the population of the towns, and part to the poor peasants. These were indeed only temporary measures of urgency, confined to certain areas, the environs of the large towns. To carry them out thoroughly the armed force of the towns would have been quite inadequate. In no case could such measures have sufficed to effect an equalisation between the rich and poor on the land, even if regularly repeated year by year. And in the last resort they might prove an effective means completely to ruin agriculture.

If private production were carried on, and its produce calculated in such wise that the producer would have taken from him everything over what was necessary for his needs, he would produce only the indispensable minimum. This is one of the reasons for the decay of agriculture in many of the countries living under Oriental despotism, in which the tax collector takes from the peasant the surplus above that which is indispensable. A similar fate is likely to overtake Russia. Socialism will effect an adjustment between economic differences by the socialisation of the means and methods of production, thus making society the owner of the products. By this means it is able to increase production to the maximum, and distribute the produce in accordance with social requirements and justice.

On the other hand, to allow private property in the means of production, and private production itself to continue, and then regularly to confiscate the surplus, leads to the ruin of production, whether it be done in the interests of an Oriental despotism or of a proletarian dictatorship. Of course in cases where such proceedings may be thought desirable as a temporary measure of urgency, this may not happen, as it may sometimes be necessary to do this. It is the reverse with the present expropriation of the well-to-do peasants. This does not alter in the least the structure of Russian society, it only introduces a new cause of unrest, and carries civil war into the domain of production, the continuance of which is so pressing a need for the Government's peace and security. Moreover, if the dictatorship of the Soviets had the will and the strength to undertake a fresh partition of the land, and to do this equitably, it would not help the peasants much, as under the present primitive methods the cultivated land in Russia would not suffice to give enough land to each peasant to raise him out of poverty.

As Massloff rightly says in the book already quoted from : " An attempt to put agriculture on the basis of equality would only be realised as a state of general poverty. To try to make all rich, while maintaining private property in the means of production is a vulgar Utopia of the lower-middle classes. If this kind of equality is not realisable, there is, on the other hand, in many countries, an equality of poverty already existing, and any extension of such a state of affairs can inspire no one. Whatever additions may be made to peasant property, there will always be too little land to permit all peasant agriculture to be prosperous. The endeavour to bring the life of the peasant into the orbit of the lower middle-class ideal, economic equality of small property, is not only Utopian, but also reactionary."

With the present numbers of the population, and the existing area of cultivation, a general raising of the social standard of the Russian peasant, cannot be accomplished by any method of partitioning the land. It can only be achieved when higher productive forms prevail, which require a general improvement in the education of the agricultural population, and a larger supply of cattle, implements, machinery, and artificial manure to be at their disposal, all of which conditions can only be introduced with difficulty and patience where small agriculture is the rule.

If the conditions necessary for intensive capitalist agriculture have only been slightly developed in Russia, and have even suffered a temporary set-back through the revolution, it is clear that the conditions for Socialist agriculture do not exist there, as they can only arise on the basis of large-scale agriculture with highly-developed technical appliances. Large-scale production can only be made to pay by technical appliances, the application of science, the most complete equipment of machinery, and the use of up-to-date methods, accompanied by a considerable division of labour. Therefore, new methods of production can only be introduced and become permanent in places where advantages can be derived, either in the form of an increased product or in that of the saving of labour. In view of the primitive appliances and the ignorance of the small Russian peasants, it is hopeless to introduce large-scale agriculture. To be sure, in Bolshevist circles, mention is made from time to time of the introduction of Socialist agriculture, after the big estates have been broken up and divided amongst the peasants. We have already referred to the theses respecting the Russian Revolution and the

tasks of the proletariat during its dictatorship in
Russia. No. 24 of these reads : " The complete
expropriation of the land owners must be now
mentioned. Land was decreed to exist for the
general good. Additional tasks are the following :
organisation of agriculture by the State, collective
working of the former big estates, association of
the small holdings into larger unities, with collective self-government (so-called agricultural communes)."

This which was said to be the task is, unfor'=
tunately, not yet fulfilled. Collective agriculture
is, for the time being, in Russia condemned to
remain on paper. Nowhere, and at no time, are
small peasants persuaded, on the ground of theory,
to go in for collective production. The Peasants'
Associations include all possible branches of
economy, and not merely the fundamental one of
cultivating the land. Small scale agriculture
necessarily creates everywhere the endeavour to
separate single plots of land from one another, and
is favourable to private property in land. Thus it
has happened in Europe and America, and the process repeats itself throughout the world. Is the
Russian peasant such an exceptional phenomenon
as to be exempt from the operation of this general
law? Whoever considers him as an ordinary man
and compares him with the peasants of the rest of

the world will declare it to be an illusion that a
Socialist economy can be built up on the basis of
present Russian agriculture.

The Revolution has only achieved in Russia what
it effected in France in 1789 and what its after-
math achieved in Germany. By the removal of the
remains of feudalism it has given stronger and
more definite expression to private property than
the latter had formerly. It has now made of the
peasants, who were formerly interested in the
overthrow of private property in land, that is, the
big estates, the most energetic defenders of the
newly-created private property in land. It has
strengthened private property in the means of
production and in the produce, which are
conditions from which capitalist production will
constantly arise, although it may be disturbed or
even destroyed for a time.

Even the poor peasants are not thinking of giving
up the principle of private property in land. Not
by collective production do they seek to improve
their lot, but by increasing their own share of land,
that is, their own private property. That thirst for
land, which always characterises the peasant, has
now, after the destruction of the big estates, made
of him the strongest defender of private property.
The peasant has shown himself to be such in all
countries where feudalism has been overcome, and

therefore he is fostered and pampered by the ruling classes as their most trustworthy defender.

This will be the most certain and lasting result of the present dictatorship of the proletariat and the poorest peasants in Russia.

The interest of the peasant in the revolution therefore dwindles so soon as his new private property is secured. He will rise against any power which would re-establish at his cost the old, large land-owners, but he has no interest in going beyond this. With his interest in the revolution will disappear his interest in his erstwhile allies, the town proletariat.

The less the peasant produces for his own need and the more he produces for the market, and is obliged to rely upon his money income, so much the greater becomes his interest in high prices for his produce. This becomes his dominating interest after feudalism has been abolished. This does not, however, bring him into antagonism to the large land-owners, whose interests are the same as his, and who become his allies, but it brings him into opposition to the non-agricultural and town population, above all, to the workers, who must spend a larger portion of their incomes upon food than the middle classes, and consequently have the greatest interest in lowering the prices of the necessaries of life.

So long as feudalism exists, the peasant and the lower classes in the towns make the best allies. This was shown in their struggles from the time of the German Peasants' War of 1525 to the time of the French Revolution of 1789. As soon as the middle-class revolution was accomplished, the peasants commenced to go over to the camp which is opposed to the town proletariat. Not only the prosperous peasants are to be found there with the big land-owners, but also the small peasants, even in democratic republics like Switzerland. The small peasants do not go over to this side all at once, but gradually, according as the traditions of feudalism become fainter, and production for the market replaces production for their own need. Even in our own ranks the idea has been cherished, which Marx also referred to in his writings on the Civil War in France, that the peasants in the coming proletarian revolution would march with the proletariat like they did in the middle-class revolutions. Even yet the Governmental Socialists are looking for an Agrarian programme which will instil in the peasants an interest in the proletarian class struggle : but, in practice, growing opposition is everywhere revealed between the proletariat and the peasants. Only those dwellers in the country have the same interest as the town prole- tariat, who are themselves proletarians, that is, who do not live by the sale of their produce, but by the sale of their labour power, by wage labour.

The victory of the proletariat depends upon the extension of wage labour in the country, which is a protracted process, a process which is slowly accomplished by the increase of large-scale agriculture, but more quickly promoted by the removal of industries to the country. At the same time, the proletarian victory depends upon the town and industrial population increasing more rapidly than the country and agricultural population. The latter is a process that goes rapidly forward. In most industrial States the country population suffers not only a relative, but an absolute decrease. In the German Empire the country population comprised 26.2 millions out of 41 millions, in 1871, that is, 64.4 per cent. of the population. In 1910 it was 25.8 out of 65 millions, or 40 per cent. The agricultural population is smaller still than the country population. When the first occupation census was taken in 1882, the agricultural population was still 19.2 out of 45.2 millions, or 42.5 per cent. of the total population. In 1907 it was only 17.7 out of 61.7 millions, or 28.7 per cent. Of these 17.7 millions only 11.6 millions were independent producers, 5.6 millions being wage-earners and the rest officials. The peasant population, therefore, only amounts to

one-sixth of the total population of the German
Empire.   On the other hand, already in 1907, the
proletariat, with about 34 millions, comprised more
than half of the population.   Since then, it has
certainly grown still more, and is not far off the
point of becoming two-thirds of the population.

The conditions in Russia are of quite another
character.   We have already shown how overwhelming is the preponderance of the peasants.
Their co-operation with the proletariat has made
possible the victory of the revolution, but it also
testifies to the middle-class character of the
revolution.   The more it is completed and
strengthened in this sense, that is, the more secure
the newly-created peasant property is made, the
more will the ground be prepared, on the one side
for capitalist agriculture, and on the other for a
growing opposition between the peasant and
proletariat.   The economic tendencies working in
this direction are all-powerful in present day
Russia, and the most forcible dictatorship would
not avail to counteract them.   Rather will it
strengthen them in the shape of a dictatorship of
the peasants.

(b) INDUSTRY.

THE industry of Russia is a different thing from
its agriculture.   Russian industry exhibits many
primitive forms, but the capitalist portion of it, just

because of its recent growth, shows its most
modern and highly-developed form.   And the
Russian industrial working class, by the side of
numerous illiterates, who come from the country
and are still limited by the narrow conceptions of
the village, contains not a few members who have
absorbed all the modern culture that is now
available to the proletariat, who are filled with the
same interest in theory which Marx praised in the
German workers half a century ago, and are distinguished by that thirst for knowledge which is
so often stifled amongst the workers of Western
Europe by the petty details inherent in democratic
conditions.

Could not a Socialist system of production be
constructed on this foundation?

This is only conceivable if Socialism means that
the workers in single factories and mines should
appropriate these themselves, in order to administer
each one separately.

Even as I write (August 5), a speech of Lenin's
in Moscow, on August 2, is just to hand, which
reports him as saying, "The workers retain
possession of the factories and the peasants will
not give back the land to the landlords."

The saying "The factories to the workers and
the land to the peasants" was recently not a social
democratic, but an anarchist-syndicalist demand.

Social democracy demanded that the factories and land should belong to society.   The individual peasant can, in case of need, work his property without any connection with other producers. The modern factory, on the other hand, stands in a network of social connections, and its isolation is inconceivable. It is not enough for the workers to take over a factory, even if they are sufficiently intelligent and trained to direct it properly.   A factory cannot run for a single day without supplies from other industries, raw material, coal, and auxiliary products of all kinds, and without the regular sale of its products.   If raw material and the mines and transport services fail, then the factory fails as well.   Its operation on Socialist lines presupposes the creation of a network of social production.   Only when society can do this, is Socialist production possible.

Social democracy does not demand the transference of factories to their workers, but strives for social production, that is, production for the needs of society in place of commodity production, and this is only possible through the social ownership of the means of production.   Even the Bolshevists have declared for the nationalisation of factories, not their transference to the hands of the workers.   The latter would only mean a change to a new form of capitalism, as experience has shown

in the numerous cases of co-operative production.
The new owners would defend their property, as
giving them a privileged position, against labourers
seeking work, whose numbers must constantly be
recruited through the insufficient share of land
falling to the peasantry.

A permanent conquest of capitalism is not
possible by giving over the factories to the workers
engaged in them, but only by transferring the
means of production to the possession of society,
that is, the whole body of consumers, for whose
need production is carried on. Thus they become
State property, or, in the case of local means of
production, belong to the commune, and eventually
also to associations of consumers.

This has even been attempted in Russia to-day.
How far it has been carried out is not yet disclosed. This side of the Soviet Republic is, in any
case, of the greatest interest for us, but, unfortunately, we are still completely in the dark.
There is, indeed, no lack of decrees, but trustworthy information concerning the operation of
the decrees is absent. Socialist production is
impossible without comprehensive, detailed, reliable
statistics, which give early information. Hitherto,
the Soviet Republic has not been able to obtain
these. What we learn about its economic effects
is highly contradictory and is not susceptible of any

verification. This is again one of the results of the dictatorship and the suppression of democracy. Where freedom of the Press and speech is lacking, there can be no central and representative body, in which all classes and parties are represented, and can express themselves, and the actua dictatorship is exposed to the temptation of only allowing to be published the information which suits it. Whether or not the dictators take advantage of this possibility, no reliance is placed on their information. This does not silence criticism, which merely seeks underground channels. It is spread by word of mouth almost as quickly as a public announcement, but without the restraint of publicity. Rumour knows no bounds. Thus, we are overwhelmed from left to right with information which is contradictory, and we are obliged to maintain an attitude of distrust towards it all.

What results have been forthcoming from the Socialist endeavours of the Soviet Government cannot, therefore, yet be estimated, not even approximately. Is it possible for it to accomplish something in this respect, which will not again be lost, but will become permanent, in the event of the Soviet Government not being able to retain its power?

That it has radically destroyed capitalism can be accepted by no one. It can certainly destroy much capitalist property, and transform many capitalists into proletarians, but this is not equivalent to the establishment of a Socialist system of production. So far as it does not succeed in doing this, capitalism will again arise, and must arise. Probably it will reappear very quickly and bring a change in the personnel of the dictatorship of the proletariat. In the place of the former capitalists, now become proletarians, will enter proletarians or intellectuals become capitalists. These people will always skim off the cream, and will remain on the side of the Government which is last on the field, and brings order out of chaos.

The Soviet Government has already been constrained to make various compromises with capital. On April 28, 1918, Lenin admitted in his before-quoted speech (reported in the News Service of the International Socialist Commission) that the expropriation of capital had proceeded too quickly : " If we are to expropriate at this pace, we shall be certain to suffer a defeat. The organisation of production under proletarian control is notoriously very much behind the expropriation of the big masses of capital."

But everything depends upon this organisation. There is nothing easier for a dictator than to expropriate. But to create a huge organism of social labour, and set it in motion, a Decree and the Red Guard will not suffice.

Even more than Russian capital, German capital will cause the Soviet Republic to recoil and recognise its claims. How far the capital of the Entente will again penetrate into Russia is still questionable. To all appearance, the dictatorship of the proletariat has only destroyed Russian capital in order to make room for German and American capital.

However this may be, it is reasonable to anticipate that the nationalisation of many branches of industry, for which the Soviet Government has paved the way, will persist, even if the Soviet Republic should be destroyed, and, after the destruction of the big estates, this will constitute the most considerable permanent achievement of the dictatorship of the proletariat.

This is all the more probable, as it is part of a movement which is going on in all modern States, even if they are capitalist. The needs of the war were responsible for it—we remember the nationalisation of the American railways—and the needs of peace will ensure its continuance.

Everywhere we must be prepared for fiscal monopoly.

But this shows that nationalisation is not yet Socialism. Whether it is so or not depends on the character of the State.

Now the Russian State is a peasant State. It is so to-day more than ever, for the peasant has now learned to make his own power felt. In Russia he is as little as elsewhere in a position to exercise his power directly in the State, as his conditions of life do not fit him for this. But he will no longer suffer the rule of any power which does not champion his interest, even if it be that of the town proletariat.

Like peasant commodity production, the State industries will also have to produce for the market, not for the State's own needs. Their most considerable market—the home one—will comprise the peasants.

Even as much as he is interested in high prices for agricultural produce, which he sells, is the peasant interested in low prices for industrial products, which he buys. As against private enterprise, it is a matter of indifference to him how these low prices come to pass, whether at the expense of labour or of profit. He has no interest in high profits for private industrial capital.

It is, however, otherwise with State industry. The higher the profits of this, the lower is the amount of revenue to be provided by taxes, which, in a peasant State, must be chiefly borne by the peasants. The peasant is accordingly as much interested in high profits for State industry as he is in low prices for its products : this means lower wages for labour.

Thus we see here another source of antagonism between peasant and industrial worker, an antagonism which will become the more marked the greater the extension which State industry undergoes.

This antagonism, and not Socialism, will be the real legacy of the Russian Revolution.

It would, nevertheless, be false to ascribe the responsibility for this to Bolshevism. Much of what they are reproached with is the necessary consequence of the conditions which confronted them, and would have disclosed itself quite as certainly under any other regime. Yet it is of the essence of dictatorship that it intensifies all existing antagonisms and raises them to their highest point.

The famine has not been created by the dictatorship, but by the mismanagement of Czarism and the war. But the fact that agriculture and the transport services have so slightly recovered in the half year following peace is the result of the civil war, which, under the dictatorship, is the only form of opposition, and is inevitable when the masses cherish lively political interest.

Again, the demobilisation of the army was a process which the Bolsheviks found going on. Yet they have prided themselves on accelerating it to the utmost, and thereby were obliged to conclude a peace which is no longer a source of satisfaction to them.

In the same way, the breaking up of the big estates among the peasants was a proceeding which had already started before the Bolsheviks seized the political power, and which, owing to the overwhelming numbers of the peasants, nobody could have hindered. Yet the dissolution of the Constituent Assembly has contributed to it, in that the last trace of social influence on the assignment of the expropriated big estates has been lost, and the partition has been left to the naked arbitrariness of the interests on the spot.

Finally, the appearance of the antagonism between peasant and industrial worker is also a phenomenon which could not be avoided, and which necessarily arises out of the prevailing economic conditions. Yet even here the Bolshevist rule has forced the growth of conditions which have sharpened and deepened the antagonism. With the dissolution of the Constituent Assembly and the demobilisation of the Army the two factors disappeared which could have furnished Russia with the quickest protection against the breaking up and partition of the land. Precisely the richest agricultural tracts of former Russia are

now detached from it. If they so remain, then
Russia will cease, especially if Siberia also
separates, to be altogether a corn or food exporting
country. The prices of the agricultural produce of
Russia will then be determined only by the home,
and not by the foreign market.

Now this is the condition in which, under
commodity production, the opposition between
peasant and industrial worker most quickly
develops. In countries which largely export
agricultural produce, the opposition between
industry and agriculture takes the form of an
antagonism of States rather than of classes, the
form of an antagonism between an industrial
State and an agricultural State. Russia, in
particular, has now, through the peace of Brest-
Litowsk, ceased to be an agricultural exporting
State, and has shaped in such a way as to promote
the most rapid and bitter economic struggle
between peasants and industrial workers.

In any case, this struggle cannot be avoided. So
much the more important is it for a far-seeing
policy to give such a form to the conditions in
which this struggle must be carried on as to make
possible to the proletariat the best development of
its strength. To lay these foundations, not only
as against capital, but also as against agriculture—
this was, during the Revolution, the most

important task of the representatives of the Russian proletariat. Nothing else than the secure establishment of democracy could have done this.

This task of the proletarian struggle for freedom, which is not less important than the institution of social production, is, in contrast to the latter, practicable in an agrarian State.

The peasants, like all sections of the working class, demand democracy. They may find themselves very well off in a democratic republic, as is shown in Switzerland and the United States But the political interests of the peasant seldom extend beyond the confines of his village, in contrast with the industrial proletarian, whose emancipation requires him to dominate the whole machinery of the State, which can be no local act. The peasant can also become enthusiastic for an emperor, who protects his property and fosters his interest, as he did in the case of Napoleon the First. The Russian peasant would oppose any return of the Czarist regime, which in his eyes was connected with the return of the old, deadly-hated landlords. But a dictator, who secured him in his property, and allowed him to devote all his attention to the cultivation of his fields and the sale of their produce, such a dictator might under circumstances be as welcome to him as the Republic. For this Dictator the way has been prepared by the suspension of Democracy, and the proclamation of the dictatorship of a class, which is in reality the dictatorship of a party, and, as Lenin himself has stated, can become the dictatorship of a single person.   In his speech of April 28 he said :

" The closer we approach the complete suppression of the middle class, the more dangerous the factor of small middle class anarchism will be for us.   The struggle against it can only be carried on by force.   If we are no anarchists, we must recognise the necessity of a State, that is a forcible transition from Capitalism to Socialism. The kind of force will be determined by the degree of the development of the revolutionary class concerned, as well as by special circumstances, such as reactionary war and the form taken by the opposition of the middle and lower middle classes. Therefore no essential contradiction can exist between the Soviet, that is, the Socialist democracy, and the exercise of dictatorial power by a single person."

In the long run nothing can be more dangerous to the Russian Proletariat than to familiarise the peasant with the idea that dictatorship, the disfranchising of all opponents, the suspension of the suffrage, and of freedom of the Press and of organisation as regards every antagonistic class, is the form of government which best corresponds to the interests of the working classes. What will then become of the town workers if they come into conflict with the enormous mass of the Russian peasants and a dictator who is recognised by them?

And what will become of the workers when their own dictatorship collapses? The alternative to the dictatorship of a party is its destruction. Dictatorship impels the party which is in possession of power to maintain it by all means, whether fair or foul, because its fall means its complete ruin.

With democracy it is quite otherwise. Democracy signifies rule of the majority, and also protection of the minority, because it means equal rights and an equal share in all political rights for everybody, to whatever class or party he may belong. The proletariat everywhere has the greatest interest in democracy. Where the proletariat represents the majority, democracy will be the machinery for its rule. Where it is in the minority, democracy constitutes its most suitable fighting arena in which to assert itself, win concessions, and develop. If a proletariat which is in a minority attains to power, in alliance with another class, through a momentary conjunction of forces, it is most short-sighted " real " politics, that is, politics of the passing moment, to endeavour to perpetuate this position by the suppression of democracy and the rights of minorities in opposition. It would destroy the ground on which alone a firm footing could be retained, after the passing of this phase, for further work and an extended struggle.

It is problematical whether the Russian proletariat has now gained more real and practical acquisitions through the decrees of the Soviet Republic than it would have gained through the Constituent Assembly, in which Socialists, even if of another colour than those in the Soviets, predominated. But it is certain that if the Soviet Republic collapses many of its achievements are likely to fall along with it.

Had the Constituent Assembly succeeded in strengthening democracy, then, at the same time, all the advantages which the industrial proletariat might have acquired by its agency would have been consolidated. To-day we rest our expectations that the Russian proletariat will not be cheated of all the fruit of the Revolution only on the supposition that the dictatorship will not succeed in stifling democratic consciousness in the Russian people, and that, after all the errors and confusions of the civil war, democracy will finally be triumphant.

Not in dictatorship, but in democracy, lies the future of the Russian proletariat.

CHAPTER X.

THE NEW THEORY.

WE have seen that the method of dictatorship does not promise good results for the proletariat, either from the standpoint of theory or from that of the special Russian conditions; nevertheless, it is understandable only in the light of these conditions.

The fight against Czarism was for a long time a fight against a system of government which had ceased to be based on the conditions prevailing, but was only maintained by naked force, and only by force was to be overthrown. This fact would easily lead to a cult of force even among the revolutionaries, and to over-estimating what could be done by the powers over them, which did not repose on the economic conditions, but on special circumstances. Accordingly, the struggle against Czarism was carried on secretly, and the method of conspiracy created the manners and the habits proper to dictatorship, and not to democracy.

The operation of these factors was, however, crossed by another consequence of the struggle against Absolutism. We have already referred to the fact that, in contradistinction to democracy, which awakens an interest for wider relations and greater objects side by side with its constant preoccupations with momentary ends, Absolutism arouses theoretical interest. There is to-day, however, only one revolutionary theory of society, that of Karl Marx.

This became the theory of Russian Socialism. Now what this theory teaches is that our desires and capabilities are limited by the material conditions, and it shows how powerless is the strongest will which would rise superior to them. It conflicted sharply with the cult of mere force, and caused the Social Democrats to recognise that definite boundaries were set to their participation in the coming Revolution, which, owing to the economic backwardness of Russia, could only be a middle-class one.

Then the second Revolution came, and suddenly brought a measure of power to the Socialists which surprised them, for this Revolution led to the complete demobilisation of the Army, which was the strongest support of property and middle class order. And at the same time as the physical support collapsed, the moral support of this order went to pieces, neither the Church nor the Intellectuals being able to maintain their pretensions. The rule devolved on the lower classes in the State, the workers and peasants, but the peasants do not form a class which is able itself to govern. They willingly permitted themselves to be led by a Proletarian Party, which promised them immediate peace, at whatever price, and immediate satisfaction of their land hunger. The masses of the proletariat rallied to the same party, which promised them peace and bread.

Thus the Bolshevist Party gained the strength which enabled it to seize political power. Did this not mean that at length the prerequisite was obtained which Marx and Engels had postulated for the coming of Socialism, viz., the conquest of political power by the proletariat? In truth, economic theory discountenanced the idea that Socialist production was realisable at once under the social conditions of Russia, and not less unfavourable to it was the practical confirmation of this theory, that the new regime in no way signified the sole rule of the proletariat, but the rule of a coalition of proletarian and peasant elements, which left each section free to behave as it liked on its own territory. The proletariat put nothing in the way of the peasants as regards the land, and the peasants put no obstacle in the way of the proletariat as regards the factories. None the less, a Socialist Party had become the ruler in a great State, for the first time in the world's history.

Certainly a colossal and, for the fighting proletariat, a glorious event.

But for what can a Socialist Party use its power except to bring about Socialism? It must at once proceed to do so, and, without thought or regard, clear out of the way all obstacles which confront it. If democracy thereby comes in conflict with the new regime, which, in spite of the great popularity which it so quickly won, cannot dispose of a majority of the votes in the Empire, then so much the worse for democracy. Then it must be replaced by dictatorship, which is all the easier to accomplish, as the people's freedom is quite a new thing in Russia, and as yet has struck no deep roots amongst the masses of the people. It was now the task of dictatorship to bring about Socialism. This object lesson must not only suffice for the elements in its own country which are still in opposition, but must also compel the proletariat of other capitalist countries to imitation, and provoke them to Revolution.

This was assuredly a train of thought of outstanding boldness and fascinating glamour for every proletarian and every Socialist. What we have struggled for during half a century, what we have so often thought ourselves to be near, what has always again evaded us, is at length going to be accomplished. No wonder that the proletarians of

all countries have hailed Bolshevism. The reality
of proletarian rule weighs heavier in the scale than
theoretical considerations. And that consciousness
of victory is still more strengthened by mutual
ignorance of the conditions of the neighbour. It is
only possible for a few to study foreign countries,
and the majority believe that in foreign countries it
is at bottom the same as with us, and when this is
not believed, very fantastic ideas about foreigners
are entertained.

Consequently, we have the convenient conception that everywhere the same Imperialism prevails,
and also the conviction of the Russian Socialists
that the political revolution is as near to the peoples
of Western Europe as it is in Russia, and, on the
other hand, the belief that the conditions necessary
for Socialism exist in Russia as they do in Western
Europe.

What happened, once the Army had been
dissolved and the Assembly had been proscribed,
was only the consequence of the step that had been
taken.

All this is very understandable, if not exactly
encouraging. On the other hand, it is not so
conceivable why our Bolshevist comrades do not
explain their measures on the ground of the
peculiar situation in Russia, and justify them in the
light of the pressure of the special circumstances,

which, according to their notions, left no choice but dictatorship or abdication. They went beyond this by formulating quite a new theory, on which they based their measures, and for which they claimed universal application.

For us the explanation of this is to be found in one of their characteristics, for which we should have great sympathy, viz., their great interest in theory.

The Bolshevists are Marxists, and have inspired the proletarian sections coming under their influence with great enthusiasm for Marxism. Their dictatorship, however, is in contradiction to the Marxist teaching that no people can overcome the obstacles offered by the successive phases of their development by a jump, or by legal enactment. How is it that they find a Marxist foundation for their proceedings?

They remembered opportunely the expression, " the dictatorship of the proletariat," which Marx used in a letter written in 1875. In so doing he had, indeed, only intended to describe a political *condition*, and not a *form of government*. Now this expression is hastily employed to designate the latter, especially as manifested in the rule of the Soviets.

Now if Marx had somewhere said that under certain circumstances things might come to a

dictatorship of the proletariat, he has described
this condition as one unavoidable for the transition
to Socialism. In fact, as he declared, almost at the
same time that in countries like England and
America a peaceful transition to Socialism was
possible, which would only be on the basis of
democracy and not of dictatorship, he has also
shown that he did not mean by dictatorship the
suspension of democracy. Yet this does not
disconcert the champions of dictatorship. As Marx
once stated that the dictatorship of the proletariat
might be unavoidable, so they announce that the
Soviet Constitution, and the disfranchising of its
opponents, was recognised by Marx himself as the
form of government corresponding to the nature of
the proletariat, and indissolubly bound up with its
rule. As such it must last as long as the rule of the
proletariat itself, and until Socialism is generally
accomplished and all class distinctions have disappeared.

In this sense dictatorship does not appear to be
a transitory emergency measure, which, so soon as
calmer times have set in, will again give place to
democracy, but as a condition for the long duration
of which we must adapt ourselves.

This interpretation is confirmed by Theses 9 and
10 respecting the Social Revolution, which state :

" (9) Hitherto, the necessity of the Dictatorship of the Proletariat was taught, without enquiring as to the form it would take. The Russian Socialist Revolution has discovered this form. It is the form of the Soviet Republic as the type of the permanent Dictatorship of the Proletariat and (in Russia) of the poorer classes of peasants. It is therefore necessary to make the following remarks. We are speaking now, not of a passing phenomenon, in the narrower sense of the word, but of a particular form of the State during the whole historical epoch. What needs now to be done is to organise a new form of the State, and this is not to be confused with special measures directed against the middle class, which are only functions of a special State organisation appropriate to the colossal tasks and struggle.

" (10) The proletarian dictatorship accordingly consists, so to speak, in a permanent state of war against the middle class. It is also quite clear that all those who cry out about the violence of the Communists completely forget what dictatorship really is. The Revolution itself is an act of naked force. The word dictatorship signifies in all languages nothing less than government by force. The class meaning of force is here important, for it furnishes the historical justification of revolutionary force. It is also quite obvious that the more difficult the situation of the Revolution becomes, the sharper the dictatorship must be.''

From the above it is also apparent that Dictatorship as a form of government is not only to be a permanent thing, but will also arise in all countries.

If in Russia now the newly-acquired general freedom is put an end to again, this must also happen after the victory of the proletariat in countries where the people's freedom is already deeply rooted, where it has existed for half a century and longer, and where the people have won it and maintained it in frequent bloody revolutions. The new theory asserts this in all earnestness. And stranger still it finds support not only amongst the workers of Russia, who still remember the yoke of the old Czardom, and now rejoice to be able to turn the handle for once, even as apprentices when they become journeymen rejoice when they may give the apprentices who come after them the drubbing they used to receive themselves—no, the new theory finds support even in old democracies like Switzerland.

Yet something stranger still and even less understandable is to come.

A complete democracy is to be found nowhere, and everywhere we have to strive after modifications and improvements. Even in Switzerland there is an agitation for the extension of the legislative powers of the people, for proportional representation and for woman suffrage. In America the power and mode of selection of the highest judges need to be very severely restricted. Far greater are the demands that should be put forward by us in the great bureaucratic and militarist States in the interests of democracy. And in the midst of these struggles, the most extreme fighters raise their heads, and say to the opponents : That which we demand for the protection of minorities, the opposition, we only want so long as we ourselves are the opposition, and in the minority.   As soon as we have become the majority, and gained the power of government, our first act will be to abolish as far as you are concerned all that we formerly demanded for ourselves, viz., franchise, freedom of Press and of organisation, etc.

The Theses respecting the Socialist Revolution are quite unequivocal on this point :

(17) " The former demands for a democratic republic, and general freedom (that is freedom for the middle classes as well) were quite correct in the epoch that is now passed, the epoch of preparation and gathering of strength.   The worker needed freedom for his Press, while the middle-class Press was noxious to him, but he could not

at this time put forward a demand for the suppression of the middle-class Press. Consequently, the proletariat demanded general freedom, even freedom for reactionary assemblies, for black labour organisations.

(18) " Now we are in the period of the direct attack on capital, the direct overthrow and destruction of the imperialist robber State, and the direct suppression of the middle class. It is therefore absolutely clear that in the present epoch the principle of defending general freedom (that is also for the counter-revolutionary middle class) is not only superfluous, but directly dangerous.

(19) " This also holds good for the Press, and the leading organisations of the social traitors. The latter have been unmasked as the active elements of the counter-revolution. They even attack with weapons the proletarian Government. Supported by former officers and the money bags of the defeated finance capital, they appear on the scene as the most energetic organisations for various conspiracies. The proletariat dictatorship is their deadly enemy. Therefore, they must be dealt with in a corresponding manner.

(20) "As regards the working class and the poor peasants, these possess the fullest freedom."

Do they really possess the fullest freedom?

The " Social Traitors " are proletarians and

Socialists, too, but they offer opposition, and are therefore to be deprived of rights like the middle-class opposition. Would we not display the liveliest anger, and fight with all our strength in any case where a middle-class government endeavoured to employ similar measures against its opposition?

Certainly we should have to do so, but our efforts would only have a laughable result if the middle-class government could refer to Socialist precepts like the foregoing, and a practice corresponding with them.

How often have we reproached the Liberals that they are different in Government from what they are in opposition, and that then they abandon all their democratic pretensions. Now the Liberals are at least sufficiently prudent to refrain from the formal abandonment of any of their democratic demands. They act according to the maxim; one does this, but does not say so.

The authors of the Theses are undeniably more honourable; whether they are wiser may be doubted. What would be thought of the wisdom of the German Social Democrats, if they openly announced that the democracy, for which they fight to-day, would be abandoned the day after victory. That they have perverted their democratic principles to their opposites, or that they have no democratic principles at all; that democracy is merely a ladder for them, up which to climb to governmental omnipotence, a ladder they will no longer need, and will push away, as soon as they have reached the top, that, in a word, they are revolutionary opportunists.

Even for the Russian revolutionaries it is a short-sighted policy of expediency, if they adopt the method of dictatorship, in order to gain power, not to save the jeopardised democracy, but in order to maintain themselves in spite of it. This is quite obvious.

On the other hand, it is less obvious why some German Social Democrats who are not yet in power, who furthermore only at the moment represent a weak opposition, accept this theory. Instead of seeing something which should be generally condemned in the method of dictatorship, and the disfranchising of large sections of the people, which at the most is only defensible as a product of the exceptional conditions prevailing in Russia, they go out of their way to praise this method as a condition which the German Social Democracy should also strive to realise.

This assertion is not only thoroughly false, it is in the highest degree destructive. If generally accepted, it would paralyse the propagandist strength of our party to the utmost, for, with the exception of a small handful of sectarian fanatics, the entire German, as also the whole proletariat of the world, is attached to the principle of general democracy.   The proletariat would angrily repudiate every thought of beginning its rule with a new privileged class, and a new disfranchised class.   It would repudiate every suggestion of coupling its demand for general rights for the whole people with a mental reservation, and in reality only strive for privileges for itself.   And not less would it repudiate the comic insinuation of solemnly declaring now that its demand for democracy is a mere deceit.

Dictatorship as a form of government in Russia is as understandable as the former anarchism of Bakunin.   But to understand it does not mean that we should recognise it; we must reject the former as decisively as the latter.   The dictatorship does not reveal itself as a resource of a Socialist Party to secure itself in the sovereignty which has been gained in opposition to the majority of the people, but only as means of grappling with tasks which are beyond its strength, and the solution of which exhausts and wears it; in doing which it only too easily compromises the ideas of Socialism itself, the progress of which it impedes rather than assists.

Happily, the failure of the dictatorship is not synonymous with a collapse of the Revolution. It would be so only if the Bolshevist dictatorship was the mere prelude to a middle-class dictatorship. The essential achievements of the Revolution will be saved, if dictatorship is opportunely replaced by democracy.

ANN ARBOR PAPERBACKS FOR THE
STUDY OF COMMUNISM AND MARXISM

For a complete list of Ann Arbor Paperback titles write:

THE UNIVERSITY OF MICHIGAN PRESS ANN ARBOR